Retire Before Mom & Dad

Glenbrook Press
P.O. Box 3591
Merrifield, VA 22116

ISBN: 978-1-7339145-0-5 (print)
ISBN: 978-1-7339145-1-2 (ebook)
ISBN: 978-1-7339145-2-9 (audiobook)

Ordering Information:
Special discounts are available on quantity purchases by corporations, associations, and others. For details, contact retirebeforemomanddad.com and rob@retirebeforemomanddad.com.

Retire
Before
Mom & Dad

THE SIMPLE NUMBERS BEHIND
A LIFETIME OF
FINANCIAL FREEDOM

ROB BERGER

To my wife, Victoria,
who stuck with me... even after that time in college when she
opened the glove box and dozens of unpaid parking tickets
spilled out. Oops.

To our children, Robert and Anna Nicole.
For the love of God, please read this book. I wrote it for you.

Disclaimer

The strategies, tactics and everything else in this book are my opinions about how to approach money, investing and life. The strategies have worked for me, and I hope they work for you. But keep in mind that this book was written for a general audience. The ideas may or may not work for you, and they may or may not work in the future.

This book is not intended to be a substitute for personalized advice from an accountant, investment advisor, or other financial professional. The publisher and author make no representation or warranty as to this book's adequacy or appropriateness for any purpose. No representation or warranty is made as to the accuracy, completeness, suitability or correctness of the material in this book. You alone bear the sole responsibility of assessing the merits and risks associated with financial decisions you make.

Contents

Part 4: Investing

Part 5: Practical Considerations

CHAPTER 1

We've Been Duped

"There is nothing more deceptive than an obvious fact."
– Arthur Conan Doyle

A young man was living a normal life. He worked in a cubicle by day and spent time on his computer at night. By all outward appearances, he was as normal as normal could be.

But something inside him said that life wasn't as it appeared. There was something not quite right in the world, but he couldn't figure out what it was. What he didn't know was that the world as he saw it was an illusion. He was being tricked into living a "normal" life so that he wouldn't discover the truth—and his potential.

That all changed when he met a guide. The guide's name, as you might have guessed, is Morpheus. And our hero's name is Neo.

In the movie *The Matrix*, Morpheus explained why Neo felt that there was more to life than meets the eye:

> The Matrix is everywhere. It is all around us, even now in this very room. You can see it when you look out your window or when you turn on your television. You can feel it when you go to work, when you go to church, when you pay your taxes. It is the world that has been pulled over your eyes to blind you from the truth.

As with Neo, the world has blinded us from the truth. In the movie, the Matrix created the illusion that the world was "normal." In our world, the deception we've come to believe about money and happiness comes from many sources. It comes from TV commercials, our parents, our friends, complete strangers, magazines, and the internet. Sometimes the lies are explicit, and sometimes they are subtle. But they never stop.

I call them "The Five Lies."

Lie #1: Financial Freedom Requires a BIG Salary

The world tells us that the average person can't achieve Financial Freedom. Unless you make a six-figure salary, are born into money, or win the lottery, you can forget about becoming a millionaire or attaining Financial Freedom. Lie #1 tells us we are destined to live paycheck-to-paycheck. This lie is easy for us to believe. Our minds play a trick on us. Let me explain.

Imagine somebody making $50,000 a year their entire adult life. Even if they saved 10 percent a year ($5,000), how could they ever become a millionaire? If they worked for 45 years, they would have saved $225,000. Sure, they may have invested their money and made some interest, but it couldn't possibly take them from $225,000 to $1 million.

Or could it?

Would you believe that it *could* take them to $3,421,620.11? That's what our $50,000 a year earner would accumulate over their working years if they invested $5,000 a year (about $416 a month) and earned an average investment return. We will explore this in depth later in the book.

Lie #2: Financial Freedom Takes 40 Years (or Longer) to Achieve

The world tells us that maybe, just maybe, and if we are lucky, we may be able to retire in our late sixties or early seventies after a lifetime of hard work. And that's only if we scrimp and save diligently, and deny ourselves life's little pleasures along the way. And it tells us that if we do achieve Financial Freedom, we'll probably be too old to enjoy it.

Once we believe Lie #2, we don't see Financial Freedom as a goal worth pursuing. Either we'll never reach the goal (Lie #1) or we'll have one foot in the grave when we do. Lie #2 sees Financial Freedom as a destination decades away.

In reality, Financial Freedom is a *journey*. And we can begin to enjoy the fruits of Financial Freedom very early in that journey.

Lie #3: Happiness is Expensive

The world tells us that true happiness is expensive. The American dream requires a big home, two fancy cars, an 80" TV, and world travel. Without this stuff, we're missing out, and we're not living life to the fullest. We hear this from the companies who, conveniently, want to sell us a big home, two fancy cars, an 80" TV, and world travel.

Lie #3 is the most pernicious of all of The Five Lies. It uses our own habits against us. We so often spend money not from deliberate choice but from the habits and routines of life. Once these habits form, they are difficult to break.

As famed investor Warren Buffett has stated, "…chains of habit are too light to be felt until they are too heavy to be broken." Once we have formed habits, changes in the way we spend money and changes in our daily routines seem painful. It feels like a sacrifice "to do without" or "to cut back." It's then that we find ourselves in the clutches of Lie #3. Like quicksand, it's difficult to escape.

Lie #4: Investing is Complicated

The world tells us that investing is complicated, confusing, risky, and scary. The investing world uses jargon that we don't understand. How can we possibly be expected to make good investing decisions any more than we should be expected to perform brain surgery?

Lie #4 may have caused you to give up. Perhaps you haven't invested in your company's retirement account. Perhaps you don't invest on your own—life is hard enough without having to worry about the stock market. Maybe you've hired somebody to help you, but you have little understanding of the important decisions they make about your financial future or how much they charge you.

What if investing were incredibly easy? Imagine creating an investment portfolio (yes, you can have an investment portfolio at any age or on any income) with just a couple of investments. Imagine spending no more than about 30 minutes a year—yes, a year—to maintain your investment portfolio.

Lie #5: Debt is a Fact of Life

Finally, the world tells us to accept debt as a fact of life. Everybody has debt.[1] Some will even tell you it's part of growing up and being a responsible adult. From school loans to car loans, credit card debt to a mortgage, debt is the way the world works.

Lie #5 makes us feel better about going into debt. Perhaps we tell ourselves that it's "good" debt, whatever that means. Combine this lie with the belief that happiness is expensive and we start to fund our lifestyle with credit cards. We decide if we can afford something according to whether we can make the monthly payment. Car salespeople even help us to make the calculation.

And then maybe, just maybe, we meet somebody who doesn't have debt. We look for signs that they are "different." Perhaps they live with their parents or

---

1 According to Northwestern Mutual, the average amount of personal debt (excluding a mortgage) was $38,000 in 2018. https://news.northwesternmutual.com/planning-and-progress-2018

in a camper.

The Five Lies combine to form a powerful grip on our lives. We convince ourselves that we can never achieve Financial Freedom on our salary. We convince ourselves that we don't want to sacrifice our happiness now in the hopes of retiring in 40 years, and we convince ourselves that happiness requires us to spend lots of money. We know we could invest *some* money but investing is complicated and we know people who have lost money instead of making money. And let's face it, a certain amount of debt helps us to fund the lifestyle that we are accustomed to.

It gets worse. Almost everybody you know believes The Five Lies. They live a life of illusion, chasing shiny things they believe will bring them happiness. They buy the next new thing and it's fun for a season. Then it's just more stuff, and they start dreaming about the next new thing.

> **Fun Fact**: According to Forbes, the average American home has grown from 1,000 square feet to 2,500. And yet, in total, Americans also spend $24 billion a year on self-storage.[2]

Because everybody around you believes The Five Lies, it's easy for you to believe them too. These lies help to make life easy. They are normal. They are comfortable. They feel like coming home after a long trip.

When your neighbor tells you about his new shiny purchase, you can tell him about yours. We even brag about how busy our lives are. How many times have you heard others say how crazy their work is? They tell you as if it's a badge of honor. And maybe you've said the same things. I know I once did. It makes us feel important...needed...part of something.

There is an expression for this: "the hedonic treadmill."

---

2   https://www.forbes.com/sites/joshuabecker/2018/11/27/why-we-buy-more-than-we-need/

The Hedonic Treadmill

We each have a *baseline* of happiness. A positive event in our lives, like getting a raise or buying a shiny new thing, may temporarily increase our level of happiness. Gradually, however, we'll return to our baseline. In other words, that cool new car you bought six months ago today is just a car. The raise you received last year is a distant memory as you fret about whether or not you'll get a raise *this* year.

You may be wondering how I know so much about the hedonic treadmill. I know because I've been there. I've run marathons on the hedonic treadmill. I'm a hedonic treadmill champion.

I did all the "right" things. I went to college and graduated with a degree and $55,000 in school loans. That was in 1992, when $55,000 bought a lot more than it does today. I went to work and spent 70 to 80 hours a week in the office and even more when I traveled for business.

I made good money and spent almost all of it. My wife and I saved a little, but we spent a lot. We bought a house, adopted two children, bought a bigger house, and took a vacation every year. Normal as normal could be.

We were on track for a typical life. I'd work until I was 65 or 70, and then we'd retire. We'd never know the life we could have had.

In 2005, everything changed. Just like Neo, I realized that there was more to life than working to consume and consuming to work. It wasn't that our lives were awful or that I hated my work. It was more about all the stuff we had brought into our lives in order to be happy—stuff that was chaining me to a life of hard labor.

I had joined a country club. We had bought fancy cars. I had bought ridiculously expensive watches for my wife and me. That's the good life, right? Yet this stuff didn't make us happier. I knew there must be *more*. Not more stuff. More life.

On June 12, 2005, I made a choice. On a piece of paper, I wrote the following: "We will be totally debt-free by June 12, 2012." Seven years.

It was a ridiculous goal. We had a big mortgage, a big home equity line of credit, my school loans, my wife's school loans, and credit card debt. If I looked just at the numbers, it was impossible for us to be debt-free in seven years.

And guess what? We failed. We weren't debt-free by June 12, 2012. But we *were* debt-free by 2016. And it was in that year that I retired from a 24-year career at the ripe old age of 49. Failure never felt so good.

In a period of just 10 years, my life had totally changed. The commitment to get out of debt led me to start a personal finance blog in 2007 (doughroller. net). And that led to a podcast ("The Dough Roller Money Podcast") and eventually to writing for Forbes. Fast forward to today and the life we have now looks nothing like the life we had before.

In 2005, I was spending two hours a day commuting to and from work in Washington, DC, and I spent 40 hours or more each week in the office. We had mountains of debt and very little savings compared to our income.

Today I'm retired from my career, and I never have to work again if I don't want to. I continue to work, however, on projects that I *love*. Oh, and my "commute" is the time it takes me to get from the bedroom to my office with a stop at the coffee pot along the way.

In *The Matrix*, Morpheus offered Neo a choice—a blue pill or a red pill.

Take the blue pill and you wake up back in your cubicle world. You'll never know the truth or your potential, but life will go on "as normal." This is what most people do, people *The Matrix* calls *blue pills*.

Take the red pill, however, and you see the world as it truly is. You may also, as it turns out, find your sense of meaning and your purpose in life.

This book is your red pill. It will open your eyes to a world of Financial Freedom you've never imagined. Are you ready to take the red pill? If you are, I promise to serve as your guide. I'll be Morpheus. You'll be Neo. You're the hero of your story. You're the Freedom Fighter.

Don't make this decision lightly. In the words of Morpheus:

> "This is your last chance. After this, there is no turning back. You take the blue pill—the story ends, and you wake up in your bed and believe whatever you want to believe. You take the red pill—you stay in Wonderland, and I show you how deep the rabbit hole goes. Remember: All I'm offering is the truth. Nothing more."

CHAPTER 2

The Game Plan

"If you don't know where you are going, you'll end up someplace else."

– Yogi Berra

You've taken the red pill. Congratulations! Welcome to a community of people I call the Freedom Fighters. Who are the Freedom Fighters? We are a growing group of people, young and old, who believe that the best thing money can buy is Financial Freedom.

In the following pages, I'll be your guide as you begin your journey. Here's our game plan.

Part 1: Your Superpower

Every hero has a superpower. Neo has superhuman abilities inside the Matrix (and in the real world too). Luke Skywalker has the force. Wonder Woman has superhuman strength.

Freedom Fighters are no different. We have a superpower too. Like Neo, Luke, and Wonder Woman, you need to: (1) understand your superpower, and (2) learn how to use it. So what's your superpower? It's something I call the Money Multiplier.

Let me give you a taste. Imagine that for every dollar you saved, your superpower enabled you to magically add $5 to it. How about $7? $10? Or to turn $225,000 into more than $3 million?

You didn't have to work for this extra money. There were no late nights or weekends in the office. And you didn't have to change your lifestyle. Save one dollar and five or more dollars are added to it.

The Money Multiplier is every Freedom Fighter's superpower. With it, you can accumulate what I call your Freedom Fund. Your Freedom Fund is the money you'll need to fund your lifestyle. It can, if you want it to, replace your job. If instead you continue to do work you love, it will enable you to live without financial worry. Without the Money Multiplier, however, you don't stand a chance of accumulating a Freedom Fund.

We learn how the Money Multiplier works in Part 1.

Part 2: Financial Freedom

In Part 2 we learn how to use the Money Multiplier to achieve Financial Freedom. We look first at what Financial Freedom is (and what it's not). Then we dive into how anybody can achieve it with the help of the Money Multiplier.

It's important to understand one thing. There are many ways to use Financial Freedom. If you are in your twenties today, you can use it to retire in your thirties or forties. If you are in your forties or fifties with little savings, you can use it to retire "on time." You can, if you choose, use what you learn in this book to work a "typical" 45-year career and retire in your sixties or seventies. (You'll have a truckload of money if you do.) You can also use your Financial Freedom to empower you to do meaningful work you love—at any age.

My job is to show you how to achieve Financial Freedom. What you do with this freedom is up to you.

Part 3: The Cost of Happiness

Part 3 is where the rubber meets the road. It's here that I show you how small changes in your daily living and spending can help propel you toward Financial Freedom. Many of the changes will not alter your lifestyle one bit. Some will change the way you live for the better.

We cover three important concepts in this section:

The Money Audit: You'll learn a simple way to save money without making major changes to the way you live.

The Power of Habits: You'll learn how your habits shape your financial future and how to develop good habits that build wealth.

The Myth of Sacrifice: What you'll learn here will empower you to make changes in your life that at first may seem like tremendous sacrifices. You'll come to learn, however, that not only were the changes not a sacrifice, they also created more meaning and opportunity in your life.

I should warn you. This is the most dangerous section of the book. It's here that we will be challenging beliefs that have been programmed into most of us for a very long time.

Part 4: AutoPilot Investing

In Part 4, we cover investing. As you'll learn, this is critical to the Money Multiplier. If this section makes you nervous, take a deep breath. We debunk a common myth that investing is complicated. I'll show you a simple and effective way to invest. We'll also offer some excellent resources that can help you along the way.

Part 4 also covers retirement accounts that can help us achieve Financial Freedom faster. They are like adding gas to an already blazing fire (thanks to the Money Multiplier). We must know, however, how to take advantage of these tools.

Part 5: Practical Considerations

Finally, we look at obstacles that may get in the way as you move toward Financial Freedom. The most common obstacle is *debt*. You may have student loans, a car payment, and/or credit card debt. How do you manage this debt load while at the same time working toward Financial Freedom? We answer this question.

Before we begin, a word of caution. Each of us has an inner voice. If yours is anything like mine, it talks to you all day, every day. Your inner voice can be brutal. In the world of money, it may tell you:

- You'll never have enough.
- You aren't smart enough to invest.
- You'll never get out of debt.
- Your parents struggled financially, and you're destined to the same fate.
- Financial freedom is for rich people, not you.
- What does the idiot writing this book know anyway (oh sorry, that was my inner voice).

And the list goes on. Eventually, you may believe and even *adopt* your inner voice.

As you read this book, your inner voice will be firing on all cylinders:

"Save how much? That's impossible."

"Invest on your own? You can't do that."

"You can try to save money, but eventually you'll fail and go back to your old ways. You always do."

I would tell you to silence your inner voice, but I know from experience that it's not that simple. Instead, recognize when your inner voice is talking to you. Acknowledge it. Remind yourself that your inner voice is not reality. And then keep reading.

Are you ready?

Let's do this.

CHAPTER 3

A Note to Mom and Dad

Dear Mom and Dad:

My name is Rob Berger. I'm the author of this book, *Retire Before Mom and Dad*. I have some good news and bad news for you.

First, the good news. Your son or daughter has taken the red pill and will be going away for a little bit. They are going on a journey that will change their lives for the better. This journey will teach them how to achieve Financial Freedom faster than they could possibly imagine.

Now to the bad news. Your child's transformation may make you jealous. As a father of two, I want the best for my children. I'm sure you want the best for your son or daughter, too. But let's face it. It will be a little hard to take when your grown child is Financially Free and you are still grinding away at the office. You should start preparing yourself emotionally for this eventuality.

Even better, why don't you join your son or daughter on their journey. What they will learn that will enable them to achieve Financial Freedom in their twenties, thirties, and forties can help you do the same thing in your fifties, sixties and seventies. If you have very little saved or even nothing at all, this book can help you get back on track. In fact, the very strategies that enable some to retire early can empower those who started late to retire "on time." It's never too late.

And besides, wouldn't it be fun if your son or daughter retired **with** mom and dad rather than **before** mom and dad? I hope you'll join us.

Best,

Rob Berger (retired at 49, and again at 51, and back to work I love at 52)

Part 1

Your
Superpower

CHAPTER 4

The Money Multiplier

"The world is full of magic things, patiently waiting for our senses to grow sharper."
– W.B. Yeats

I made a promise to you. I promised that you have a superpower. It's something I call the Money Multiplier. If used correctly, it can bring in far more money than you or I could ever save without it. Ignore the Money Multiplier and you'll never achieve Financial Freedom.

To understand this superpower, we must change the way we see our money. Most people see each dollar that enters their lives and nothing more than that—a dollar. What they don't see is the dollar's potential.

Imagine winning the lottery. I'm not talking about a $5 scratcher. I'm talking about a million-dollar jackpot. You bought the ticket. You've got the ticket in your possession. Every. Single. Number. Hits. Bam! You're a millionaire.

Now imagine you never check the ticket. You bought it a few days before the drawing and then forgot about it. There it sits in the center console of your car collecting dust. Tired of the clutter a few weeks later, you gather up all the trash, including the wadded-up ticket, toss it into an empty McDonald's bag, and throw it away.

You *were* a millionaire. But not now. Why? Because you didn't know the value of that lottery ticket when you picked it up and threw it away.

Ridiculous story, right? Well, I'm sorry to break it to you but most people do the exact same thing with their money. The difference is, they don't throw the million dollars away all at once. They do it dollar by dollar, day by day, over a lifetime. Why? Because they never appreciate the awesome power they hold in their hands every time they earn a dollar.

Fun Fact: Unclaimed lottery tickets are a real phenomenon. According to CNN, $2 billion in lottery tickets go unclaimed every year.[3] As I type these words, there is a Mega Millions ticket worth $1.5 billion unclaimed in South Carolina. It expires in 2019.[4]

We have a choice every time a dollar passes through our hands. We can either spend it or we can put it to work. Spending money is, of course, necessary. We spend money for true needs, like housing, food, and clothing. We also spend money on wants, like cable TV, expensive cars, and gym memberships. I'm not making a judgment here. I have cable TV, an expensive car, and a gym membership. But these are *wants*, not needs.

As for those dollars we don't spend, we can put them to work for us. We put our dollars to work when we deposit them in a savings account. We put them to work when we invest in a 401(k) or IRA. And we even put them to work when we pay down high-interest debt.

Every dollar we put to work is like an employee.

They are the best kind of employee. They never complain about the working conditions. They don't ask for a raise. They never sleep or ask for time off. They work 24/7. And if we let them, they will keep working for us for the rest of our lives. Like the energizer bunny, they just keeping going, and going, and going.

It gets better.

Our dollars can be as popular as the king and queen of the prom. Put them to work in the right way and they attract more dollars. Then these new "em-

---

3   http://money.cnn.com/2014/11/02/technology/mobile/2-billion-unclaimed-lottery-prizes/
4   https://www.wfmynews2.com/article/news/mega-millions-15-billion-jackpot-still-unclaimed/83-da9417f8-5881-47af-88b8-ad824940c302

ployees" come into our lives without any work on our part.

At first, the new dollars trickle in. You hardly notice the interest from a savings account or small dividend payments from a mutual fund. But let them work alongside the dollars you have earned and something magical happens. The dollars you have worked for and saved earn more dollars, which also earn more dollars, which in turn earn *more* dollars. What started out as a simple savings account or 401(k) turns into real wealth and true Financial Freedom.

Let's get our hands dirty with some numbers.

Using the Money Multiplier, anybody making an average income over their working years can easily—yes, easily—become a millionaire. In this example, we're actually going to make it much, much harder.

We'll assume you make $50,000 a year. That's a lot of money. So let's make things a bit more difficult. We'll further assume the following:

- You never get a raise. Ever. You make $50,000 a year for the rest of your life.
- The most you can save is 5%. That comes to about $208 a month ($208.33 to be precise, but we'll stick with $208).
- You work and save your money for 45 years (from age 22 until you retire at 67).
- You can't invest the money you save, so instead you stuff it under your mattress.

That last assumption is ridiculous, of course. What this does is remove the Money Multiplier from the equation. It takes away your superpower. It makes you like everybody else who believes The Five Lies. We'll bring the Money Multiplier back in a minute, but for now, let's act like most people in the world and pretend we don't have a superpower.

So how much money will you have under your mattress when you retire at the ripe old age of 67?

$112,320 ($208 x 12 months x 45 years).

Not only are you not a millionaire, you don't have enough to retire. And we haven't even considered inflation. Because you aren't investing your money, the only way you can do better is to increase your savings. But even if you double your savings to 10%, the results aren't even close to $1 million.

Doubling your savings to 10% would enable you to save $224,640. That's not so bad today; however, 45 years from now, $224,640 won't buy nearly as much as it will today, thanks to inflation.

Let's now introduce the Money Multiplier into the equation. Let's assume you invest your money in a mutual fund. (Don't be intimidated by investing, even if you aren't sure what a mutual fund is—we'll cover that later in the book.)

We'll assume you earn a 9.3%[5] annual return on your investments. So how much will you have if you save 5% of your income, or $208 a month?

Before we look at the numbers, let's review:

Without investing your money, you'll end up with $112,320 under your mattress after 45 years. The only change we are going to make is to *invest* your money. This change doesn't require you to:

- Work overtime;
- Stay at the office on weekends to keep the boss happy;
- Get a second job;
- Cut out vacations;
- Eat rice and beans every day;
- Win the lottery;
- Or, as in our example, get a raise.

Just invest your money.

So now to the results. Your nest egg would grow from $112,320 to...

Are you sitting down? $1,708,072.76.

---

5   I love people who read footnotes. Some of the best material ends up at the bottom of the page. Footnote readers, I've found, are also skeptics by nature. I know because I *am* one. You're down here because you question the 9.3% return assumption. You wonder what's up with the .3%. Why not just 9% or 10%? And you may question whether a 9.3% annual return is realistic. Good for you. You *should* question it. We'll be looking at return assumptions a lot in this book. Until then, the number came from Vanguard, a mutual fund company. Since the 1920s, an investment portfolio of 70% stocks and 30% bonds has earned an average annual return of 9.3%.

(Source: https://personal.vanguard.com/us/insights/saving-investing/model-portfolio-allocations?lang=en)

Think about it. You worked hard and saved $112,320 over your working years. By investing your money wisely, you added another $1,595,752.76 to your wealth.

> Work hard and save: $112,320
> Invest and enjoy life: $1,595,752.76
> Total: $1,708,072.76

Of your total wealth, about 6.5% of it came directly from your savings. More than 93% of your wealth in this example came from the *compounding* of your investment returns. Now you know why I call it the Money Multiplier and why it's your *superpower*.

Video: I've created a series of videos covering many of the topics in this book. The videos are screencasts, allowing you to look over my shoulder at my computer as I walk through many of the concepts that I cover. For example, you'll find a video about the numbers and calculations in this chapter at https://www.retirebeforemomanddad. com/Chapter4. You'll find links to the videos at the end of each chapter where a video would help explain the concepts covered.

There are two important things to learn from this example:

First, our minds do not intuitively grasp the power of compounding (which is what the Money Multiplier is). Ask most people making $50,000 a year if they could become millionaires without ever getting a raise and saving just 5% of their income and the answer will be a resounding "NO WAY!"

Why? We compare the $208 a month in savings to $1 million. It's like standing on the streets of New York City looking up at the Empire State Building and wondering how to get to the top without using the elevators or stairs. Impossible. But the compounding of our investments enables us to achieve what seems like the impossible.

Second, wealth comes from investment returns, not directly from saving money. We must save to get the ball rolling, of course. But the vast majority of wealth comes from investment returns. That's true for you and me, and it's true for the richest men and women in the world.

That's not to say that the amount of money we save isn't important. Part 2 of this book covers saving money in detail. But don't compare what you save to your ultimate goal. It's like comparing a snowball to an avalanche. One leads to the other, but they couldn't be more different.

Have you ever been in an airport with a moving walkway? It's like an escalator that moves you forward rather than up or down. The Money Multiplier is a moving walkway for your money. And the longer you let your money ride, the faster the moving walkway goes.

This brings us back to looking at your dollars as potential employees. In this case, over 45 years of your working life, you put 112,320 "employees" to work by spending less than you made. They worked hard, earned a 9.3% return, and brought into your life 14x more wealth—$1,595,752.76.

That's the superpower of the Money Multiplier.

Why am I driving home the power of compounding? If I told a young adult that they could build $1.7 million in wealth, they'd think I was crazy. Without realizing it, they'd compare the $1.7 million to what they were earning. By that comparison, it *is* crazy. Somebody making say $50,000 a year can't fathom $1.7 million in wealth.

We need to see the connection between $208 a month and $1.7 million over a lifetime. Once we understand that connection, $1.7 million is no longer crazy. It's just compounding.

In the next few chapters we are going to tear down and rebuild the Money Multiplier. We need to know how it works so that we can use this superpower in our own lives. The Money Multiplier is as simple as simple can be. It has only three components: Amount, Time, and Return.

3 KEY CONCEPTS

1. We don't intuitively grasp the power of compounding, or what I call *the Money Multiplier*.

2. The Money Multiplier consists of just three parts: Amount, Time, and Money.

3. By understanding how the Money Multiplier can generate far more wealth than our savings alone, we take the first step towards a lifetime of Financial Freedom.

Let's start with Time.

CHAPTER 5

Tick-Tock

"Lost time is never found again."

– Benjamin Franklin

CNN recently reported the sale of a penny for $1.2 million.[6] As you might imagine, this was no ordinary penny. The coin is known as the "Birch Cent," and it was struck in 1792 (incidentally, that's the year my children think I was born).

Now at first glance, the sale is extraordinary. Imagine starting with a penny and turning it into over $1 million. Sure, it took 225 years, but it started out as a penny for goodness sake. Of course, one might chalk this up to the crazy world of numismatics. Surely you couldn't invest your way from one cent to $1.2 million, even if you did have 225 years.

Oh really? Let's do the math.

If we assume a 9.3% return, guess how much one cent would be worth after 225 years.

Result: $4,892,563.14 (compounded annually).

Imagine a family passing that penny down from generation to generation and then selling it 225 years later for $1.2 million. They would have been better off if their ancestor had invested it in 1792 rather than holding onto it. By a country mile. In this case, a penny earned is $4,892,563.14 saved.

Given the length of time involved, every variable is critical. Just change the

6 http://money.cnn.com/2015/03/27/news/first-u-s-penny-auction/

compounding from annual to monthly, and the result jumps from $4.8 million to over $11 million.

And that brings me to the first part of the Money Multiplier—time. To see the power of compounding in action, you must give it time. In our example from the previous chapter, we assumed an investment period of 45 years. I've chosen that time period because it mirrors, more or less, our traditional working years. Yet we shouldn't overlook the fact that 45 years is a really long time.

To put that time period into perspective, 45 years ago:

- Gerald Ford was president after Richard Nixon resigned from office;
- Inflation was 11.3% in the U.S.;
- The Dow closed at 616;
- A gallon of gas cost 53 cents;
- Muhammad Ali defeated George Foreman by knockout in the 8th round in a fight known as the *Rumble in the Jungle*;
- Stephen King published his first novel, *Carrie*;
- Leonardo DiCaprio was born;
- *The Sting* won best picture; and
- Many of you reading this book had not yet been born.

The point: 45 years is a long, long time.

Imagine a college professor assigning a paper that was due in 45 years. I suspect most students wouldn't rush back to their dorm to get started. They might wait a year or two…or ten.

That's a problem when it comes to investing.

Let's return to our example of investing $208 a month earning 9.3%. Recall that over 45 years the investment snowballs into $1,708,072.76.

Now let's imagine we delayed investing for just one year. Instead of 45 years of investing, we socked $208 a month away for 44 years. That's only about $2,500 less, right?

Not exactly.

Remember compounding? That $2,500 we didn't invest in year one ended up costing us $153,504.54. I know—it seems impossible. But it's true. Reducing our investment time period from 45 to 44 years reduces our nest egg from $1.7 million to $1.55 million. The reason is that we lose that last year of compounding returns, at a time when our balance is over $1.5 million. That last year alone would have generated our $153,504.54 at a 9.3% return.

The problem, of course, is not just one year. Those who consistently invest over a 44-year period should do just fine in retirement. (Although losing $153,504.54 is nothing to sneeze at.) The problem is when we delay *even longer*.

Delay for more than a year and the losses get much worse:

Delay 5 years: Lose $643,197.40.
Delay 10 years: Lose $1,047,937.16.
Delay 15 years: Lose $1,302,624.55.
Delay 20 years: Lose $1,462,889.69.

The compounding that helped us build an avalanche of wealth works to multiply the losses for those who delay.

Let's look at time from another perspective. Let's compare one person who saves and invests for 10 years with another person who saves and invests for 35 years. Who ends up with more money?

If that seems like a trick question, it is. We are going to let the 10-year investor, who we'll call Samantha, start today. Imagine she's graduated from college, started her first job, and signed up for her company's 401(k) retirement account.

The 35-year investor, who we'll call William, doesn't start investing until the first 10 years are up. William waits for 10 years for no good reason. Investing just didn't seem important to William when he started his job.

During this entire time, Samantha keeps her money invested. After year 10, however, she can't add any additional savings to her account. Given that they both earn our average return rate of 9.3%, who ends up with more money?

I confess that when I did these calculations, I didn't believe them at first. So I double checked and triple checked my math. My editor even checked it.

Samantha ends up with $40,940.80 after 10 years. Remember that she invested $208 a month for 10 years, earning a 9.3% annual return. Here's where things get crazy. She stopped saving additional money and just let her investments continue to compound. Thirty-five years later she was a millionaire. Her nest egg was worth $1,047,937.16.

What about William, our 35-year investor who has to wait 10 years before he can get started? He didn't do as well. His wealth added up to $660,135.60.

Let's review.

> Samantha saved a total of $24,960 ($208/month x 12 months x 10 years). William saved 3.5 times as much, or $87,360 ($208/month x 12 months x 35 years). Because he got a late start, however, he still ended up with just 63% of the wealth Samantha achieved.

The moral of the story? Start saving and investing today. Don't let your superpower waste away.

Here you may be asking about *early retirement*. After all, the title of this book promises that you can retire before your mom and dad. Forty-five years won't get the job done. Or perhaps you are in your forties or fifties (hello, mom and dad; glad you joined us) and don't have another 45 years to work and save.

Fair point. It's in Part 2 that we'll dig into just *how quickly* you can achieve Financial Freedom. But here I use traditional notions of retirement to show how time affects the Money Multiplier.

Remember, as important as time is, it's only *one* of the three components of the Money Multiplier. In the next chapter, we will cover the second key aspect of the Money Multiplier—The Amount.

3 KEY TAKEAWAYS

1. The best time to start saving and investing is today.

2. Delaying even one year can cost you thousands of dollars over the long run. Delay for five, 10, or 15 years and the losses really add up.

3. If you are late to the game, there is still hope. Will there be tough choices ahead? You bet. But you've got this. Keep reading.

Video: https://www.retirebeforemomanddad.com/Chapter5

CHAPTER 6

Think Small

"Be faithful in small things because it is in them that your strength lies."
— Mother Teresa

My mom is a retired teacher who continues to serve as a substitute teacher several days a week. Her students love her, even though she's tough as nails. On many occasions, she has shown up at a student's house uninvited to talk to parents about why their child isn't doing his or her homework. Yikes!

She has an interesting way to save money. She pays cash for just about everything. But when a $5 bill comes her way, she saves it; she will not spend a fiver. They all go into savings. Five dollars isn't much money, but she is able to save thousands of dollars with this little trick.

In this chapter we are going to look at the Amount component of our Money Multiplier. Like my mom's habit of saving every $5 bill, we'll see how even small amounts of money can have a big effect on our wealth. Let's start with the example we've used in the previous chapters.

Recall that saving $208 a month for 45 years at a 9.3% return generates more than $1.7 million in wealth. Recall also that $208 a month is roughly 5% of our hypothetical $50,000 a year salary.

What if we rounded down? What if, instead of saving $208 a month, you saved $200. It's only eight bucks a month. The equivalent of two lattes, perhaps. How big a difference could it possibly make?

$65,695.11

That's what it would cost you over your working years by making that small, insignificant change to the amount you save.

What if instead of rounding down to $200, you rounded up to $225 a month? How much **more** would you have at retirement?

$139,602.10

Small amounts of money, invested over time, turn into piles of cash, thanks to the Money Multiplier.

In both of the above examples, we looked at the effect of small changes to your savings over a long period of time—45 years. Let's take it a step further and look at how saving relatively small amounts of money can build wealth over shorter time periods.

And that brings me to the **Rule of 752**.

I learned about this rule in late 2013. I had just started my podcast and I invited a guy who goes by the name of Mr. Money Mustache to be a guest on the show. His story is as simple as it is compelling.

He retired at age 30. Let that sink in for a moment. He didn't inherit money. He didn't win the lottery. He's not a professional athlete or a Hollywood actor. He's an engineer. Well, he *was* an engineer until he retired.

He started working full time in 1997 after finishing a computer engineering degree. His annual salary was $41,000. A few years later, his wife graduated and landed a job where she was making $44,000 a year. Then, over time they received raises. For 10 years, Mr. Money Mustache and his wife saved and invested. While the amounts varied, at one point he saved roughly 60% of his income.[7] One thing he shared with me during the interview was the Rule of 752. (You can listen to the podcast here: https://www.retirebeforemomanddad. com/MMM.)

Here's how it works. Take any recurring **weekly** expense that you have and multiply it by 752. The result is how much you would have if, instead of spending the money, you invested it for 10 years earning a 7% return. There's no magic here in the number 752. It's the result of the Money Multiplier applied

---

7   http://www.mrmoneymustache.com/2011/09/15/a-brief-history-of-the-stash-how-we-saved-from-zero-to-retirement-in-ten-years/

to a weekly expense and assuming a 7% return.

I want to make one modification to this rule. Rather than assuming a 7% return, let's stick with our 9.3% return assumption. As mentioned earlier, I'm using that return because it's the average return, over the past 90 years, of a portfolio consisting of 70% stocks and 30% bonds. (Don't worry if terms like "portfolio," "stocks," or "bonds" make your head spin. We'll cover all of that in Part 4 of the book.)

By making this seemingly small change, however, our rule changes from the Rule of 752 to the **Rule of 857**. That should give you a hint as to just how important our rate of return is. Let's take the Rule of 857 for a spin. Keep in mind that the expenses below are per week:

- Latte 3x a week $4 ($12 x 857): $10,284
- Cable TV $25/week ($25 x 857): $21,425
- Eating out 2x a week ($30 x 857): $25,710
- More car than you need ($40 x 857): $34,280
- More house/apartment than you need ($50 x 857): $42,850

All of the above ($157 x 857): **$134,549.**

These numbers get crazy big when you think about a 45-year time period. Over 45 years we need to use the Rule of 36,036.

- Latte 3x a week $4 ($12 x 36,036): $432,432
- Cable TV $25/week ($25 x 36,036): $900,900
- Eating out 2x a week ($30 x 36,036): $1,081,080
- More car than you need ($40 x 36,036): $1,441,440
- More house/apartment than you need ($50 x 36,036): $1,801,800[8]

All of the above ($157 a week x 36,036): **$5,657,652.**

---

8   If you've been paying close attention to the numbers, you've spotted what looks like an error. Our $208 a month generated just over $1.7 million after 45 years. Yet here, $50 a week generates $1.8 million. What gives? Two things. First there are about 4.3 weeks on average per month. Thus, saving $50 a week comes out to about $217 a month. Second, in this example, I compounded interest weekly because we are looking at weekly expenses. In the earlier examples, I compounded interest monthly. As you can see, seemingly small changes can have major consequences given enough time.

At this point you have every right to ask one of the most important questions you can ever ask.

So what?

When I talk to my children about these numbers, they typically roll their eyes. It's not that they don't believe the numbers. Numbers are numbers. It's that all they hear me saying is that they should stop living now so that maybe in 45 years they can retire.

We cover this very topic in Part 3—The Cost of Happiness. Until then, keep a few things in mind.

The "so what" is not that you should give up lattes or cable or eating out. The "so what" is not that you should move to a cheaper apartment or home, or downgrade your car. And the "so what" is not even about retirement 20 years or even 45 years from now.

The "so what" is that small amounts of money, invested over time, turn into large piles of cash that can change your life. The "so what" is that you can build wealth over time if you choose to make some very simple choices. The "so what" is that the changes you can make won't make you less happy, even though you may think they will at first.

We've been conditioned to believe that there's no point in investing small amounts of money. We now know that this is *a lie*. Small amounts of money, invested over time, can change your life.

That's a fact. What you do with this reality is up to you. Remember, I'm just your humble guide. You're the Freedom Fighter.

3 KEY TAKEAWAYS

1. Small changes in the amount you save and invest have big consequences over time.

2. Seemingly insignificant changes in how you spend money on a weekly basis can go a long way to helping you achieve Financial Freedom.

3. You don't need a lot of money to start investing. As you'll learn, even $25 a month will get you started.

Video: https://www.retirebeforemomanddad.com/Chapter6

CHAPTER 7

Investment Returns

"Long-term compounding is an investor's best friend, so why get in its way."

– Guy Spier

The year was 1494, two years after Christopher Columbus sailed the ocean blue. This story, however, involves a different Italian by the name of Luca Pacioli, a mathematician. In that year, Pacioli published a book on mathematics called the *Summa de arithmetica, geometria, proportioni et proportionalita* (Summary of arithmetic, geometry, proportions, and proportionality.)

In his work he describes what has become known as the **Rule of 72**. Here's what he wrote:

"In wanting to know of any capital, at a given yearly percentage, in how many years it will double adding the interest to the capital, keep as a rule [the number] 72 in mind, which you will always divide by the interest, and what results, in that many years it will be doubled. Example: When the interest is 6 percent per year, I say that one divides 72 by 6; 12 results, and in 12 years the capital will be doubled."[9]

The Rule of 72 enables us to estimate how long it will take to double our money given a certain interest rate. The higher the interest rate, the faster we can double an initial investment. Lower the interest rate and doubling our money takes longer.

Here's how it works. We divide our expected rate of return on our invest-

---

9   https://en.wikipedia.org/wiki/Rule_of_72#History

ments into 72. The result is an estimate of how many years it will take us to double our initial investment. For example, if we earn 7% annual interest on an investment, it will take us about 10 years to double our money (72/7 = 10.2 years). Earn 9% interest, and the time to double our money shrinks to about eight years (72/9 = 8).

The Rule of 72 doesn't account for additional investments. It assumes you invest one lump sum of money at the start. Still, it gives us a glimpse into the power of the Money Multiplier. The difference between 7% and 9% interest may not seem like much, yet at 9% we double our money in eight years rather than 10. Multiply this over a lifetime of investing and the difference grows exponentially.

Over a 40-year period, for example, an initial investment will double four times at a 7% rate of return (once every 10 years), while it will double five times with a 9% return (once every eight years). That means that a $10,000 initial investment will grow to about $160,000 at 7%, but $320,000 at 9%. Yeah, a 2% difference in your rate of return is kind of a big deal.

Let's take a closer look. We've assumed that our investments earn 9.3% on average each year. Why 9.3%? The number comes from Vanguard, a mutual fund company. According to Vanguard, from 1926 to 2017, an investment portfolio of 70% stocks and 30% bonds has returned on average 9.3% a year.[10]

There are three important takeaways. First, I didn't just make up the number. Second, a portfolio of 70/30 stocks to bonds is a reasonable investing approach (more about this later). And third, just because this portfolio has returned 9.3% since 1926 doesn't mean it will return 9.3% in the future.

It's that last point we need to explore. Let's imagine that instead of 9.3%, a 70/30 portfolio returned 9.0% over our lifetimes. Would losing 0.3% of our return make much of a difference?

Recall from the Money Multiplier chapter that investing $208 a month for 45 years at a 9.3% return nets us $1,708,072.76. If we reduce our investment returns by just 0.3%, our wealth shrinks to: $1,540,214.12.

That seemingly minuscule change in our investment returns, multiplied over

---

10 https://personal.vanguard.com/us/insights/saving-investing/model-portfolio-allocations

our working years, reduces our wealth by **$167,858.04**.

Now let's imagine a big change in returns. We'll assume that instead of earning 9.3%, we earn 8.3%. Perhaps the market didn't do as well as we hoped. Perhaps we got scared when the market was falling and took some of our money out just before the market went back up. Perhaps we paid an advisor 1% of our investments to manage them. Whatever happened, we earned an average of 8.3% on our Freedom Fund.

The first thing to note is that a change of 1% in our investment returns is huge. It's easy to see a 1% difference in returns as insignificant. Many banks offer about 1% interest on savings accounts. Many credit cards offer 1% cash back or even more. How big a deal could losing 1% on our returns really be?

Here are the numbers: Instead of accumulating a Freedom Fund of more than $1.7 million, that "small" 1% difference lowered our Freedom Fund to $1,213,503.86. We lost **$494,568.90**.

The rate of return on our investments matters. A lot. And seemingly small changes, multiplied over time, will have a huge, life-changing effect on our Freedom Fund.

We'll come back to investment returns in Part 4, AutoPilot Investing.

Let's review. We've looked at how Time, Amount, and Return come together to create the Money Multiplier. We've seen how even small changes in each can have a big effect on our wealth. That's good news. Like a tiny seed that grows into a mighty oak tree, small decisions we make today will supercharge our finances down the road.

3 KEY TAKEAWAYS

1. The Rule of 72 offers an easy way to determine how long it will take you to double your money. It also gives us a glimpse into the importance of our investment returns.

2. Small changes in investment returns, even "just" 0.3%, will, over the long run, have major effects on your wealth.

3. Larger changes in investment returns, such as 1%, will have life-changing effects on your money.

Video: https://www.retirebeforemomanddad.com/Chapter7

Part 2

Financial Freedom

CHAPTER 8

Financial Freedom

"The secret to happiness is freedom.... And the secret to freedom is courage."
– Thucydides

This book is about the simple numbers behind a lifetime of Financial Freedom. It seems sensible to examine what Financial Freedom is. What does it look like? What does it feel like?

Let's first look at what Financial Freedom is *not*.

It's not a fat paycheck. I've met many people who make a six-figure salary and struggle financially. They wouldn't know Financial Freedom if it walked up to them and slapped them in the face. They struggle to make their big mortgage payment. They struggle with expensive car lease payments. They have no money in the bank. They look rich. But behind the veneer is a lot of financial pain. In Texas they'd say, "Big hat, no cattle."

It's not a big house. One of the most insidious lies we've been told is that owning a home is the American Dream. This fallacy has caused families to spend a lifetime paying the mortgage on a home they couldn't afford. There is, of course, nothing wrong with owning a home. I own a home. But too much of a good thing can be bad. And there's nothing wrong with renting. Financial Freedom is not about whether you rent or own, or how big your house is.

It's not the shiny things we can buy. Along with a big house, many spend their money on expensive cars, clothes, jewelry, and gadgets. That's why they need such a big house. They look rich. They act rich. They impress their neighbors. They look happy on Facebook and Instagram.

Here's what you don't see. You don't see them freaking out about how they will make their monthly payments. Who posts Instagram pictures of that? You don't see them stress out at work because they may not get their quarterly bonus. You don't see them lying awake at night worried sick that their financial house of cards could come tumbling down at any moment.

So what is Financial Freedom? Ultimate Financial Freedom comes when you can live off of your savings and investments without the need to work. It's as simple as that.

For most people that sounds impossible. Even those nearing retirement age question just how they will survive financially. It's here we need to see Financial Freedom as a journey, not a destination.

And that brings me to what I call the 7 Levels of Financial Freedom.

As you'll see, the 7 Levels are based on your *expenses*, not your income. This is critical to understand. We are conditioned to define financial success based on a fat paycheck. Yet Financial Freedom hinges on how much you *spend*, not how much you make.

Thus, the more you spend, the more it takes to reach each level of Financial Freedom. And the less you spend, the easier it is to reach each level. Lowering your expenses is like lowering the hurdles in an Olympic race. It makes reaching Financial Freedom easier.

With that, let's look at the 7 Levels of Financial Freedom.

Level 1: 1 month of Expenses Saved

Level 1 might not seem like Financial Freedom but it's an important start to our journey. It's here that you stop living paycheck to paycheck. You may only have a one-month cushion, but that's a big deal. It gives you breathing room for *when*—not *if*—the unexpected happens.

Studies show that most people cannot come up with $400 for an emergency. According to a study by the Federal Reserve, 4 in 10 Americans couldn't cover a

$400 emergency with their savings.[11] In other words, most Americans have not achieved Level 1 Financial Freedom.

Level 2: 3 Months of Expenses Saved

At Level 2, we reach what most financial gurus say is the minimum emergency fund you should have. You now have enough money in the bank to handle most emergencies. The money could even help you survive during a short-term job transition.

Level 3: 6 Months of Expenses Saved

Level 3 is time for celebration. You've maxed out your emergency fund. You've got breathing room to handle emergencies and even several months of unemployment. It's at Level 3 that you've also gained some confidence. It takes commitment to save six months of expenses. It requires discipline and persistence. If you can reach Level 3, you can reach Level 7.

Level 4: 1 Year of Expenses Saved

Level 4 is when things start to get interesting. Two things happen:

First, with one year of expenses saved, you can handle a significant bout of unemployment. Today the average person will change jobs 12 times during their lifetime.[12] While we hope these transitions go smoothly, Level 4 Financial Freedom will help you ride out any bumps in the road.

Second, we start to see the benefits of the Money Multiplier. As we now know, most of our Freedom Fund doesn't come from putting aside money each month. That's how it starts, of course, when we are trying to reach Level 1, 2,

---

11 https://www.federalreserve.gov/publications/2018-economic-well-being-of-us-households-
    in-2017-dealing-with-unexpected-expenses.htm

12 https://www.thebalancecareers.com/how-often-do-people-change-jobs-2060467

or even 3. Eventually, however, the money we save starts to earn a nice return. In fact, if done right, our investments will produce far more income than our jobs. That takes time, and it's here at Level 4 that we start to get a glimpse of the power of the Money Multiplier.

Let's return to our hypothetical $50,000 a year salary. We'll assume we spend $45,000 of this salary each year, saving the remaining $5,000. That means to reach Level 4 Financial Freedom we need to have saved $45,000 (one year of expenses). As we continue to invest our Freedom Fund and earn a 9.3% return on average each year, our $45,000 Freedom Fund will generate $4,185 over the next 12 months. That's nearly as much as we are saving each year from our paychecks. That's the Money Multiplier in action.

Level 5: 5 Years of Expenses Saved

At Level 5, you've already exceeded the savings that most will achieve in a lifetime. Assuming $50,000 in annual expenses (the round number makes the math easier), for example, you've amassed $250,000 in savings and investments. At a 9.3% return, your Freedom Fund will generate almost $25,000 in returns over the next 12 months. In other words, your investments are generating income approaching 50% of your annual spending.

Level 5 also represents a danger point. It's here that some may become complacent. With so much money saved, it's easy to return to old habits or to lose focus. Knowing that *now* will help you avoid this danger when you reach Level 5.

At this point you may be wondering what Level 5 Financial Freedom feels like. After all, one could say this is nothing more than traditional retirement savings. Oh, but it's so much more.

Let me tell you a story.

In the middle of my career, I had a job that at times was very unpleasant. I have a vivid memory of a meeting with the boss. He was yelling at an employee on the phone. He was out of line. It was then I understood the true power of Financial Freedom.

While my wife and I hadn't reached Level 7 at that time, we were right around Level 5. I knew I could walk out of that job if I needed to and we'd be fine financially. I wasn't stuck. And it was a great feeling.

Less than a year later, I took a pay cut to pursue a new opportunity. I took that risk because I could; I wasn't chained to my job or to the salary. It turned out to be the best career move of my life. And it was made possible because of Level 5 Financial Freedom.

This is an example of how money saved and never spent can have a profound effect on our lives.

Level 6: 10 Years of Expenses Saved

Level 6 is an important milestone. It's here that your investment income will begin to equal and then exceed how much you are spending each year.

Let's again assume you spend $50,000 a year. At Level 6, you will have a Freedom Fund totaling $500,000. A 9.3% return will generate returns of $46,500 over the next 12 months, bringing your Freedom Fund to $546,500. The following year, with a Freedom Fund totaling almost $550,000, you will on average generate just over $50,000 a year.

Talk about a great feeling. You are working hard, earning an income, and spending $50,000 a year. At the same time, your Freedom Fund is generating returns equaling the same amount. Like a snowball rolling downhill, your wealth is multiplying before your very eyes.

Level 7: 25 Years of Expenses Saved

Level 7 is the Ultimate Financial Freedom. It's here that you can completely retire from work if you so choose. Or, if you're like me, you can work on projects you love while still earning an income. The choice is yours.

Level 7 enabled me to retire from the practice of law at 49. Following my retirement, I continued to run my personal finance blog, newsletter, and podcast. Two years later, I sold my blog but I still record a podcast each month, and

I'm a Deputy Editor at Forbes. These activities generate income. But I do them because I'm passionate about personal finance and investing.

When you reach Level 7, you can pursue your passions. That may mean keeping your job. There's nothing wrong with that if that's what you love. It may mean starting a business. Here's the point—you decide for yourself what you'll do when you reach Level 7. It's a beautiful feeling.

The remainder of this book will show you how to reach Level 7 Financial Freedom. We'll walk through the numbers, how long it takes, and some tips on how to get you there faster.

Before we move on, however, there are some important observations we need to make about the 7 Levels of Financial Freedom.

First, Financial Freedom is a journey, not a destination. Unlike traditional retirement savings, you can enjoy the fruits of Financial Freedom as early as Level 1. As your Freedom Fund grows, it empowers you to make decisions based on what's important and meaningful to you. It gives you the freedom to take chances you might not otherwise take.

Second, the 7 Levels enable you to monitor your progress. Knowing that you are moving in the right direction toward your goals is motivating. Known as The Progress Principle, which we will examine later, it tells us that making progress toward any goal gives us the grit to keep going. The 7 Levels give us a concrete way to measure that progress.

Third, Financial Freedom has nothing to do with your income. The 7 Levels are the same whether you are a teacher making $40,000 a year or LeBron James making $50 million. How long it takes you to reach each level depends entirely on what percentage of your income you spend and save, not how much you make. A teacher saving 10% of her income will reach Level 7 in the exact same number of years as it would take LeBron James if he saved 10% of his salary (trust me for now; I'll show you the numbers soon).

That's not to say that income is irrelevant. But Financial Freedom is first and foremost about our expenses, not our income. That explains the all too common stories we hear about celebrities, athletes, and lottery winners going broke. They had huge incomes, yet they failed to achieve lasting Financial Freedom. Why? Their expenses consumed all of their income and then some.

Fourth, the levels of Financial Freedom do not include anything about debt. That may surprise you. How can you have Financial Freedom with a mountain of credit card debt? The answer is, you probably can't. But we need to understand why.

Monthly debt payments increase our expenses. As our expenses increase, it becomes harder and harder to reach each level of Financial Freedom. Let's look at an example.

Let's assume that between credit card debt, car loans, and school loans, you pay $1,000 a month toward debt. That $1,000 payment translates directly into how much you need saved for each level of Financial Freedom. Focusing just on this $1,000 monthly debt payment, here's what you need at each level:

Level 1: $1,000
Level 2: $3,000
Level 3: $6,000
Level 4: $12,000
Level 5: $60,000
Level 6: $120,000
Level 7: $300,000

And these numbers do not include any of your other monthly expenses. Do these debt payments make reaching Level 7 Financial Freedom impossible? No. It's also not impossible to swim with an anchor wrapped around your neck. But it sure is difficult. And the heavier the anchor—the bigger the debt payments—the harder it gets. Eventually you sink.

There is good news, however. As you pay off debts, your monthly expenses go down. In the above example, once you've paid off all of those debts, the amount you need for Level 7 Financial Freedom drops by $300,000. Not only that but you now have an extra $1,000 a month that was going to debt payments to put toward your Freedom Fund.

Fifth, you reach Level 7 Financial Freedom when you have saved 25 years of expenses. What's so special about having 25x our annual expenses? The answer has to do with what's called the 4% rule.

Developed by financial planner William Bengen in the early 1990s, the 4% rule is a guideline on how much of our Freedom Fund we can spend each year without running out of money. It was developed with retirees in mind, but we can use it here as well.

If you spend $50,000 a year, you'll reach Level 7 when you have saved $1,250,000 ($50,000 x 25). Four percent of $1,250,000 just happens to equal – you guessed it – $50,000. We'll examine the 4% rule shortly.

Sixth, the 7 Levels give us a compelling framework with which to understand decisions we make in our everyday financial lives. Remember the Rule of 857? It's a shorthand way to see how small savings can grow with the Money Multiplier. It's a great way to see the power of compounding. But it doesn't tell us anything about Financial Freedom. The Level 7 framework does.

As you'll see in later chapters, you can use the 7 Levels of Financial Freedom framework to understand how daily, weekly, and monthly decisions affect the time it will take you to reach each level of financial freedom.

Seventh, the levels of Financial Freedom are not spaced out evenly. The first three levels are just a few months of expenses apart. The difference between Levels 6 and 7 is 15 years. What gives?

What if I told you that the time it takes to get to Level 5 is about the same time it will take you to go from Level 6 to Level 7? I know, it seems impossible. How can saving five years of expenses (Level 5) take as long as saving an extra 15 years of expenses (the difference between Levels 6 and 7)?

The answer is the Money Multiplier. When you are starting out on your journey to Financial Freedom, most of your Freedom Fund is the result of what you've saved. The Money Multiplier hasn't had time to work its magic.

Imagine saving $5,000 over the course of a year. Assuming our 9.3% rate of return, you will earn $465 on these savings over the next 12 months, bringing your balance to $5,465 (not including any additional savings). Not bad, but the majority of this amount came from your savings, not from investment returns.

Now fast forward 10 years. If you kept saving $5,000 a year at a 9.3% return, your Freedom Fund would have grown to $82,012.83. Over the next 12 months, the Money Multiplier will generate an additional $7,627.19. That's more than your $5,000 in annual savings. And that's why Levels 5, 6, and 7 are spaced so far apart yet don't take more time to reach than lower levels. They have the benefit of the Money Multiplier.

Finally, mom and dad, or anybody retiring say at 65 or older, have some distinct advantages. You'll have the benefit of social security and Medicare. You may also have a pension or other retirement income. These have a direct effect on Level 7 Financial Freedom.

Imagine you want $60,000 a year of income during retirement. Without social security, for example, you would need to amass approximately $1.5 million ($60,000 x 25). With say $20,000 a year from social security, however, you need only generate $40,000 a year in income from your investments. That brings the total nest egg down to $1 million ($40,000 x 25).

In the next chapter we'll begin to examine how the Money Multiplier and 7 Levels of Financial Freedom can help us answer THE question—how much should *you* save?

3 KEY TAKEAWAYS

1. Financial Freedom is about how much you *spend*, not how much you make.

2. Achieving Financial Freedom is a journey, not a destination. The benefits of Financial Freedom can be felt as early as Level 1.

3. The Money Multiplier is the superpower that propels us to Level 7 Financial Freedom.

Take Action: Determine your current level of Financial Freedom. This will require you to know, or to find out, how much you spend each month. Be sure to include periodic expenses, such as gifts and vacations. For your savings, do not include short-term savings you plan to spend on a specific goal, such as buying a home or a car.

Video: In this video, I show you a free calculator that I created to help you examine and understand the 7 Levels of Financial Freedom (https://www.retirebeforemomanddad.com/Chapter8).

CHAPTER 9

How Much Should You Save?

"Yeah, 220, 221. Whatever it takes."

– Jack Butler

In the 1983 movie *Mr. Mom*, Jack Butler (played by the incomparable Michael Keaton) was going through a bit of a midlife crisis. He had just lost his job and his wife returned to work to support the family. And the wife's new boss, Ron Richardson, was taking her on a business trip.

Jack was a bit insecure about his wife taking a trip with Ron. When Ron stopped by the house to pick up Jack's wife for the trip, Jack answered the door doing exactly what I would have done. He was wearing goggles and revving a chain saw in Ron's face.

When the commotion died down, Jack explained to Ron that he was adding a wing on to the house, including rewiring it. Ron innocently asked if the wiring would be 220, to which Jack responded, "Yeah, 220, 221. Whatever it takes."

I think about this movie whenever somebody asks me how much they should save. I want to say "20, 30%, whatever it takes." However, the problem with the question is that there is no one "right" answer. More importantly, people often choose a saving rate without understanding the consequences of their decision. Let me show you what I mean.

The traditional approach to the question of how much you should save is to rely on a rule of thumb. Here are three common rules of thumb:

- **Save 10%**: Saving 10% was popularized by the book, *The Richest Man in Babylon,* by George S. Clason. Originally published in 1926, it shows that by saving 10% of every dollar that comes into your life, you'll do just fine. It was true in 1926. It's still true today.
- **Save 15%**: Not to be outdone, the popular Dave Ramsey espouses saving 15% of your income. Remember, he does everything with gazelle-like intensity. In one podcast, Dave stressed that there is nothing magical about 15%. The key is to get serious about saving for retirement.
- **Save 20%**: Before Senator Warren was a senator, she wrote a book about personal finance. In her book, *All Your Worth: The Ultimate Lifetime Money Plan*, she talks about the 50/20/30 budget—50% of our income should go to needs, 30% to wants, and 20% to savings.

There is nothing wrong with any of these rules of thumb. Save even ten percent and you are doing better than the vast majority of people. (The average saving rate in the U.S. is around 6%, according to the Fed.[13]) But that leaves us with a big question: what should YOU do?

Should you be average and save 6%? Should you ratchet up your savings to 10%? 15%? 20%? Or some other saving rate?

The rest of this section of the book will help you answer this question for yourself. And the following section will give you tips on how to actually *do* it. Let's start with understanding just how different the above rules of thumb are over a lifetime of saving.

How much would we have after 45 years, using the above saving rates, if we made $50,000 a year and earned a 9.3% return? Using the same math we've already discussed, here are the numbers:

Save 10% ($5,000) -- $3,421,620.11
Save 15% ($7,500) -- $5,132,430.17
Save 20% ($10,000) -- $6,843,240.22

---

13 https://fred.stlouisfed.org/series/PSAVERT

As you can see, there's a huge difference between saving 10% and 15%, and an even bigger difference at 20%.

While these numbers are impressive, by themselves they don't help us answer how much we should save. To begin to answer that question, we need to understand two related concepts: Saving Rate and Spending Rate. We'll cover both of these in the next chapter. But first, one more thing to consider about rules of thumb.

Rules of thumb fail to account for your specific situation. There is no single rule of thumb that applies equally to a 22-year-old computer programmer just out of college and a 55-year-old divorcee with no money saved.

Rules of thumb can be a helpful guide. They can point us in the right direction. We should not, however, blindly follow them. We should never follow any rule of thumb without understanding the implications of our decision.

In the next chapter I'll give you the tools you need to decide for yourself how much you should be saving.

3 KEY CONCEPTS

1. There are many reasonable rules of thumb when it comes to how much you should save.

2. Rules of thumb can be a good starting point.

3. We should always think for ourselves, making informed decisions about our finances.

Video: https://www.retirebeforemomanddad.com/Chapter9

CHAPTER 10

Emergencies

*"There is only one kind of shock worse than the totally unexpected:
the expected for which one has refused to prepare."*

– Mary Renault, *The Charioteer*

In the last chapter, we looked at three rules of thumb when it comes to savings—save 10%, 15% or 20% of your income. We are going to apply these heuristics to the 7 Levels of Financial Freedom. It's only when we see how different Saving Rates affect our journey to Financial Freedom that we can make an *informed* decision about how much to save.

To accomplish our goal, I need to point out the obvious. If you save ten percent of your income, you spend 90%. If you save 15%, you spend 85%. And if you save 20%, you spend 80%. The more you save, the less you spend. Obvious, I know. But the sliding scale relationship between our Spending Rate and our Saving Rate is important.

To understand how this sliding scale relationship works, let's apply it to saving for emergencies. The general rule of thumb (yes, another rule of thumb) says we should save three to six months' worth of expenses. For now, let's figure out how long it will take to save just *one* month of expenses.

The answer depends on your Saving Rate and your Spending Rate. Let's compare two individuals who both make $5,000 a month after taxes. The first person, we'll call him Frank, saves 10%, or $500 a month, and spends 90%, or $4,500 a month. The second person, we'll call her Stephanie, saves 20%, or

$1,000 a month, and spends 80%, or $4,000 a month.

To summarize:

Frank
Saving Rate: 10% ($500/month)
Spending Rate: 90% ($4,500/month)

Stephanie
Saving Rate: 20% ($1,000/month)
Spending Rate: 80% ($4,000/month)

To save one month's worth of expenses, Frank needs to save $4,500. Stephanie, on the other hand, only needs to save $4,000. Because she spends less money, her goal of saving a month of expenses is easier to achieve than Frank's. At the same time, she's saving more money each month toward the goal. It's as if they are running a race, and Stephanie is both faster than Frank and doesn't have to run as far. She'll win every time hands down.

Let's look at the numbers. To calculate how long it takes to save one month of expenses, you divide your Spending Rate by your Saving Rate.

Here is the formula: Spending Rate/Saving Rate = Time to Save One Month of Expenses

Now let's return to Frank and Stephanie. Recall that Frank has a Saving Rate of 10%. If Frank saves 10% of his income, he'll build up a one-month emergency fund in nine months (90/10 = 9). As for Stephanie, she will save one month of expenses in just four months (80/20 = 4).

Notice that it takes Frank just over twice as long as Stephanie to save one month of expenses. Why isn't it exactly twice as long, given that Stephanie is saving twice as much? When our Saving Rate goes to 20%, our Spending Rate goes down to 80%. Not only are we saving *more* but we need to save *less* money to equal one month of expenses.

Recall from the Apollo 13 mission that NASA used the Slingshot Effect to safely bring home three astronauts. Apollo 13 launched on April 11, 1970 on a mission to the moon. The moon landing was aborted two days later, however, when an oxygen tank exploded. Despite the loss of cabin heat, limited oxygen, a shortage of drinking water, and a crippled ship, Apollo 13 landed safely back to Earth six days after launch. To get the crew home, NASA executed a circum-lunar trajectory, using the moon's gravity to slingshot the ship back to Earth.

We use the same concept to propel our finances toward Financial Freedom. Every dollar we don't spend increases our savings. But just as importantly, it decreases how much we need in our Freedom Fund to reach each level of Financial Freedom. The Slingshot Effect.

The effect of spending less as our Saving Rate rises can be seen even more clearly the more we save. Based on the following Saving Rates, here's how long it will take to reach Level 1 (one month of expenses saved):

5% Saving Rate-->19 months
10% Saving Rate-->9 months
15% Saving Rate-->5.7 months
20% Saving Rate-->4 months
25% Saving Rate-->3 months
30% Saving Rate-->2.3 months
35% Saving Rate-->1.9 months
40% Saving Rate-->1.5 months
45% Saving Rate-->1.2 months
50% Saving Rate-->1 month

This is a perfect example of why you should look at money from a long-term perspective. For those that save 5% of their income, it will take them 9.5 years to save an emergency fund of six months of expenses (Level 3). *9.5 years.* Save 20% and you reach Level 3 in just *two years.* Save 30% and it drops to about *one year.*

In the next chapter we'll explore in more detail how your Saving Rate (and by extension your Spending Rate) can help you achieve Level 7 Financial Freedom. Specifically, we'll be taking a closer look at the 4% rule. Armed with this information, you can decide for yourself how much you should save, rather than relying on somebody else's rule of thumb.

To give you a taste, it will take Frank—or anybody else who has a 10%

Saving Rate—about 43 years to reach Level 7. Stephanie will reach the same goal in just 30 years—13 years faster.

3 KEY CONCEPTS

1. The more you save, the less you spend.

2. The less you spend, the faster you can achieve each level of Financial Freedom, thanks to the Slingshot Effect.

3. Your Saving Rate, and by extension your Spending Rate, is the key to unlocking a lifetime of Financial Freedom, as we will explore in more detail in the next chapter.

Take Action: Calculate your current Saving Rate and Spending Rate. Be sure to include money you are contributing to a 401(k), 403(b), or other workplace retirement plan as part of your Saving Rate. You'll be using this information in the next chapter.

CHAPTER 11

The 4% Rule

"And thirdly, the Code is more what you'd call guidelines than actual rules. Welcome aboard the Black Pearl, Miss Turner."

– Captain Hector Barbossa (*Pirates of the Caribbean*)

Everything we've talked about thus far leads to this critical chapter. It's here that we see just how the magic of the Money Multiplier, coupled with a healthy Saving Rate, can produce Level 7 Financial Freedom. It's also how you can decide for yourself just how much money you should save each month (how you'll actually save it is the subject of the next section of the book).

Recall that we achieve Level 7 Financial Freedom when we've accumulated 25 years of expenses in our Freedom Fund. In this chapter we are going to look at why this works and how long it takes to get there. It's extremely easy to estimate how long it will take anybody to reach Level 7. We just need three pieces of information:

1. Saving Rate
2. Return on Investments
3. Withdrawal Rate

You're already familiar with Saving Rate and Return on Investments. Your Saving Rate is the percentage of your gross income (before taxes[14]) that you

---

14 I use gross income throughout most of the book. If most of your Freedom Fund is in Roth retirement accounts, however, feel free to use after-tax income in your calculations. Why?

save. So far we've assumed a 9.3% return rate. That's fine for understanding the Money Multiplier. As we now turn to estimating how long it will take to achieve Financial Freedom, however, we need to make an important adjustment. We need to account for inflation. Why? Because over time the cost of everything from shelter to clothing to food goes up.

Over the past 100 years or so, inflation has averaged just under 3%. Therefore, we will reduce our assumed 9.3% return (called a nominal return because it's not adjusted for inflation) by 3%. The resulting 6.3% is referred to as the "real" rate of return because it is adjusted for inflation.

Keep in mind that there are no guarantees. I'm using these numbers based on how the markets and inflation have behaved since 1926. How they will behave in the future is anybody's guess.

Going forward I'll still use the nominal return, 9.3%, for some purposes in this book. But when it comes to estimating the time it takes to reach Level 7 Financial Freedom, I'll always use 6.3%, the real rate of return.

The Withdrawal Rate refers to how much we plan to take out of our Freedom Fund each year once we retire. And that brings us to something called the 4% Rule. The rule is designed to provide an easy way to determine how much of your nest egg you can spend each year without running out of money. As the name of the rule suggests, in year one you can spend 4% of your investments. In each year following, you adjust the amount you spent the previous year by the rate of inflation.

It's not guaranteed that your money will last in retirement, as this depends in part on other factors such as actual investment returns and inflation. In the words of Captain Barbossa, think of it more as the 4% Guideline than the 4% Rule. But it's considered a reasonably safe approach to retirement spending. To put it bluntly, the 4% Rule gives us a reasonable chance of dying before our money runs out.

As noted earlier, financial planner William Bengen first wrote about the 4% rule in 1994.[15] Then three professors at Trinity University conducted what

Because you'll pay no taxes on the money in a Roth 401(k) or IRA when you withdraw the money in retirement.

15 http://www.retailinvestor.org/pdf/Bengen1.pdf

has become known as the Trinity Study.[16] The 1998 study further supported Bengen's findings.

At first glance, 4% might seem low. We are assuming a nominal rate of return of 9.3%. If that's a reasonable assumption, what happens to the other 5.3%? Good question. Keep in mind three things:

1. **We must account for inflation**. By earning more than we spend with our investments, we can reinvest the difference to help our portfolio keep pace with rising prices.

2. **We must account for stock market declines**. While we are assuming a nominal rate of return of 9.3%, actual stock market returns are lumpy. Some years you might earn 25%, but in others you might lose 25%. Our portfolio must have the ability to withstand extreme bear markets.

3. **Finally, we must account for a more conservative portfolio**. We are assuming a stock to bond allocation of 70/30. Once you retire, however, it's common for some to increase their allocation to bonds to make their portfolio less volatile. If we move to a 60/40 or even 50/50 portfolio, our expected nominal return falls below 9.3% (more on all of this in the section on Investing).

Let's use the 4% Rule in our Level 7 Financial Freedom calculation. Take the amount of money you need to live on each year and divide it by 4%. The result is how much you need in your Freedom Fund to reach Level 7 Financial Freedom.

Let's look at some examples:

$30,000 / 4% = $750,000
$50,000 / 4% = $1,250,000
$75,000 / 4% = $1,875,000
$100,000 / 4% = $2,500,000

---

16 https://afcpe.org/assets/pdf/vol1014.pdf

By the way, you get the same result by multiplying your expenses by 25.

$30,000 x 25 = $750,000
$50,000 x 25 = $1,250,000
$75,000 x 25 = $1,875,000
$100,000 x 25 = $2,500,000

Before we go to the next step, one important observation is in order. We've assumed a 4% withdrawal rate. That's a really important assumption. As we lower the withdrawal rate assumption, the amount we need in our Freedom Fund to achieve Level 7 Financial Freedom goes up. And as we raise the withdrawal rate, what we need in our Freedom Fund to achieve Level 7 Financial Freedom goes down. That may seem counterintuitive.

Think of it this way. The amount we need to live on is fixed in these calculations. If for *you* it's $50,000 a year, that doesn't change based on the withdrawal rate you assume. And if you assume a 3% withdrawal rate, you'll need a larger nest egg to generate $50,000 in income than if you could take out 5% in year one.

The numbers help us to see this more clearly:

$50,000 / 3% = $1,666,667
$50,000 / 4% = $1,250,000
$50,000 / 5% = $1,000,000

The withdrawal rate makes a serious difference in these calculations. And that raises an important question. Should you ever assume something other than 4%? While I believe 4% is a reasonable assumption for most people, particularly for setting our Freedom Fund goal, extreme cases do exist.

For example, if your goal is to retire at 30 and never earn another dime doing anything the rest of your life, 3 or 3.5% is a better assumption. Why? Because your money needs to support you for upwards of 60 years or more. If your goal is to work until you are 80, you could probably assume a 5% withdrawal rate or even much higher. After all, even if you live to 100, you've only got 20 years in retirement. Again, these are extreme cases.

Also, we haven't accounted for other sources of income, such as social security or a pension. For our purposes, we'll stick with 4%.

Let's use the following example:

- Annual Income: $75,000
- Saving Rate: 20% ($15,000 a year)
- Spending Rate: 80% ($60,000 a year)

An individual planning to spend $60,000 a year (including taxes) would need to accumulate $1,500,000 ($60,000 / 4% or $60,000 x 25 if you prefer) in order to reach Level 7 Financial Freedom.

Now take a moment to calculate *your* number. Take your gross income, subtract how much you save, and multiply what remains by 25.

Once we know our Freedom Fund goal, we can estimate how long it will take to reach that goal based on our Saving Rate, rate of return, and current savings. The math here is easy, but to make it even easier, I've created a spreadsheet that does the work for you.

It's a Google Docs spreadsheet that you can view here: https://www.retire beforemomanddad.com/FFCalc. I walk through the spreadsheet in the video that accompanies this chapter. Note too that the spreadsheet allows you to account for your current savings and any matching contributions your employer makes to your 401(k) or other workplace retirement account.

Using this spreadsheet, we can estimate that it will take about 31 years to reach Level 7 in the above hypothetical. I've assumed a 6.3% average real rate of return and no savings at the start.

There are several aspects of the spreadsheet, which I call the Financial Freedom Calculator, worth noting:

Income Is Irrelevant: How much you make doesn't change the results. The length of time it takes to achieve Level 7 Financial Freedom is a function of the percentage of income you save, the rate of return, and the withdrawal rate. If two people each save 10% of their income and earn the same rate of return, it will take them the same length of time to reach Level 7, even if one makes $50,000 a year and the other $500,000.

If this seems impossible, remember that the person making $500,000 and saving 10% is spending $450,000 a year. Yes, they are saving a lot more than the person earning $50,000 a year. But they need a Freedom Fund of $11,250,000 ($450,000 x 25).

Save More, Spend Less: The more we save, the less we spend. As our Saving Rate goes up, it impacts our years to Financial Freedom in two important ways. The first is that we save more, growing our investments faster. The second effect is equally important – we spend less. Because we spend less, the amount of money we need to reach each level of Financial Freedom goes down. This is the Slingshot Effect we looked at earlier.

Every Percent Counts: The results are very sensitive to the rate of return. For example, a person saving 10% of his income will need 50 years to reach Level 7 assuming a 5% real return on investments. Increase the real rate of return to 6.3% and the time to reach Level 7 Financial Freedom drops to 43 years. **A one percent difference in investment returns can add five years or more to the time it will take you to reach Level 7**.

I can hear you now, "Rob, this is all just dandy, but you haven't answered my question. How much should I be saving?" Great question. And now you can answer that question for yourself.

With this approach, you can set your Saving Rate based on your goals. A 25-year-old, for example, wanting to achieve Level 7 in about 20 years and assuming a real rate of return of 6.3%, will need to save 35% of his income. Yes, saving 30% of one's income is not an easy feat. Of course, achieving Level 7 Financial Freedom at age 45 may provide ample motivation.

Some folks, when presented with this data, still want guidance on how much to save. If pushed, my answer is always "at least 20%." In the next section of the book, we'll look at concrete ways you can make this a reality. In the next chapter, we'll look more closely at the relationship between our Saving Rate and Level 7 Financial Freedom.

3 KEY CONCEPTS

1. The 4% Rule helps us estimate how much we need in our Freedom Fund to reach Level 7 Financial Freedom.

2. To determine how long it will take us to reach Level 7, all we need are our Saving Rate, Investment Return, and Withdrawal Rate.

3. Our time to Level 7 is very sensitive to changes in our Investment Returns and Withdrawal Rate assumption.

Video: https://www.retirebeforemomanddad.com/Chapter11

CHAPTER 12

Level 7 & Saving Rate

"Money often costs too much."

– Ralph Waldo Emerson

The beautiful thing about the Money Multiplier is that small changes can have a big effect on your journey to Level 7. And *big* changes can have a huge effect.

Let's first look at some big changes. Then we'll turn to small changes.

Big Changes to Saving Rate

So far, we've assumed the following:

- Annual Income: $75,000
- Saving Rate: 20% ($15,000 a year)
- Spending Rate: 80% ($60,000 a year)

We know that it will take about 31 years to reach Level 7 Financial Freedom assuming a 6.3% after inflation investment return. We also know that the results don't change with a higher or lower income if your Saving Rate remains at 20%.

But what if we change the Saving Rate in a significant way? For example, let's assume we decrease our Saving Rate to 10%. Here's what the new numbers look like:

- Annual Income: $75,000
- Saving Rate: 10% ($7,500 a year)
- Spending Rate: 90% ($67,500 a year)

When we multiple our annual spending ($67,500) by 25, the result is $1,687,500. Thus, we are saving less (now just 10% or $7,500) and we have to accumulate more ($1.69 million instead of $1.5 million). This is like the Slingshot Effect in reverse. The result is that it will take us nearly 12 years longer to reach Level 7 (43 years instead of 31). You can use the Financial Freedom Calculator to see for yourself (http://www.retirebeforemomanddad. com/FFCalc).

This is an example of a big change to our Saving Rate having a huge effect on our lives. If we increase our saving rate to 30%, however, we get the opposite result. Here are the numbers:

- Annual Income: $75,000
- Saving Rate: 30% ($22,500 a year)
- Spending Rate: 70% ($52,500 a year)

Because our Spending Rate has gone down, the amount we need to accumulate in our Freedom Fund has fallen to $1,321,500 ($52,500 x 25). Assuming a 6.3% real rate of return, our time to Level 7 drops from 31 years to about 25 years.

Here's approximately how long it will take to reach Level 7 Financial Freedom assuming a 6.3% after inflation investment return based on various Saving Rates:

5% Saving Rate --> 55 years
10% Saving Rate-->43 years
15% Saving Rate-->36 years
20% Saving Rate-->32 years
25% Saving Rate-->28 years
30% Saving Rate-->25 years
35% Saving Rate-->22 years
40% Saving Rate-->19 years

45% Saving Rate-->17 years

50% Saving Rate-->15 years

The above assumes we started with no savings. (The Financial Freedom Calculator mentioned above allows you to include your current savings in the calculation.) It also assumes we spend as much before retirement as we do after. It's true that some costs likely will go down, such as costs associated with our job (e.g., clothing, commuting) and our children. It's also true that some costs may go up, such as healthcare.

The point is not to calculate Level 7 to the penny. That's impossible, particularly if you have many years ahead of you before reaching this goal. Rather, the point is to empower you to make an informed choice about how much you want to save. The answer for you might be one of the rules of thumb we've talked about. That's fine. But now you are making an informed decision with the big picture in mind.

Small Changes to Saving Rate

Now let's look at how smaller changes to our Saving Rate can affect our years to Level 7 Financial Freedom. Let's start with something known as the Latte Factor. It's a concept popularized by personal finance author David Bach. The concept is simple. Instead of buying a latte every day, invest the money. Why? **Small amounts of money, invested over time, turn into piles of cash**. We saw this in action with the Rule of 857.

It's an important point. Too often we view wealth as requiring us to have thousands of dollars to invest. If all we have is a few bucks a day, what's the point? The Latte Factor assumes that we forego our daily latte. Assuming our beverage of choice costs $5, that frees up about $150 a month to save and invest. If we earned a 9.3% nominal return over 45 years, we'd accumulate...

$1,231,783.24.

Believe it or not, there's some bad news in that number. The bad news is that we have no excuses. Each of us has the power to save and invest for our future. Extreme circumstances may prevent us from saving for a period of time. Sudden unemployment or soul-crushing student loans come to mind. Apart from these and similar situations, which are temporary (one hopes), we have no excuses.

Now to the real question. How does applying the Latte Factor affect our journey to Level 7 Financial Freedom?

Recall that saving 20% of our $75,000 annual income enables us to reach Level 7 in about 31 years. What if we increased our Saving Rate by $150 a month?

We were saving $15,000 a year, or $1,250 a month. By increasing this monthly amount by $150 to $1,400 a month, we increase our annual savings to $16,800, or 22.4%.

Let's not forget the Slingshot Effect. By increasing our Saving Rate from 20% to 22.4%, we decreased our Spending Rate from 80% to 77.6%.

Here's what the new numbers look like:

- Annual Income: $75,000
- Saving Rate: 22.4% ($16,800 a year)
- Spending Rate: 77.6% ($58,200 a year)

At first glance it may not seem like much. And in one way it's not. It's just a daily $5 latte. But look what happens when we multiply $58,200 by 25: the result is $1,455,000.

Instead of a Freedom Fund of $1,500,000, our goal has decreased by $45,000. And at the same time, we've increased our annual savings by $1,800 ($150 x 12). The Slingshot Effect.

And this one little change allows us to reach Level 7 sooner. Instead of Level 7 taking about 31 years at a 6.3% real return, we reach it in about 29 years. In other words, by making this one small change, we shaved more than two years off the time it will take to reach Level 7 Financial Freedom.

Now let's address some objections.

First, some tell me that life is short. We should live for the day. What's the point in foregoing a cup of coffee for more than 30 years? We may die long before then.

It's an important point. And I'm not here to tell you to stop drinking lattes, watching Netflix, or taking vacations. What I am here to tell you is that **the best thing money can buy is Financial Freedom**. With each dollar that comes into your life, use a portion of it to buy your freedom. With what's left over, drink as many lattes as your heart desires. In other words…

Freedom First, Lattes Second

Furthermore, the point isn't to pick on lattes. You can apply this concept to any regular expense. We'll come back to this idea when we cover what I call the One-N-Done System for Saving Money.

Now to the second objection. I've assumed an individual makes $75,000 a year. What if you make $300,000 a year? Saving on a $5 a day latte habit won't have nearly the same effect on your Level 7 journey.

In our example above, saving an extra $150 a month increased our Saving Rate from 20% to 22.4%. That's a significant jump. At $300,000 a year, however, an extra $150 a month in savings increases our Saving Rate from 20% to 20.6%. While any increase in your Saving Rate is a move in the right direction, it won't have the same effect.

There are several things to keep in mind. First, it's a good problem to have. If you are bringing in $300,000 a year, you're doing very well and should be able to save far more than 20%. Second, those with more income typically have the ability to find more ways to save. Going from a Saving Rate of 20% to 23% on a $25,000 a month income would require increasing savings from $5,000 to $5,750. That may require foregoing more than a latte, but it's still not extreme savings given the income.

Finally, regardless of your income, saving $150 a month at 9.3% nominal return for 45 years still generates more than $1.2 million in wealth.

Start thinking now about how you can make small changes in your daily habits and routines that could save small amounts of money. We'll return to this topic in the next section of the book.

3 KEY CONCEPTS

1. Our Saving Rate has a direct effect on how quickly we can achieve Financial Freedom.

2. Every dollar we save has a Slingshot Effect—it increases our savings *and* it decreases our Freedom Fund goal.

3. Even small changes to our Saving Rate will have a big impact on our journey to Level 7.

Part 3

Buying Your Freedom

CHAPTER 13

The Cost of Happiness

"If more of us valued food and cheer and song above hoarded gold,
it would be a merrier world."

– J.R.R. Tolkien

What makes you happy?

It's a simple question. It's also one of the hardest questions in life to answer. In fact, many live their entire lives without ever answering this question.

Before reading any further, answer this question for yourself. What makes you happy? List the top 10 things in your life that make you the happiest. We'll come back to that list in a moment.

Now ask yourself how much income you need to make in order to be happy. A recent analysis published in the *Nature Human Behaviour* journal concluded that emotional happiness occurs with an income between $60,000 and $75,000.[17] The results are consistent with past research that pegs what I call the Happiness Income at $75,000.

But these studies answer the wrong question.

We shouldn't be asking how much we need to **make** to be happy. We should be asking how much we need to **spend** to be happy.

Now go back to your list. How many items on your list cost money? How many are free? How do they align with how you spend your money and your

---

17 https://www.nature.com/articles/s41562-017-0277-0

time?

I want to share a story with you.

This story is about two people, Don and Wendy. They were acquaintances in college, occasionally taking the same classes. They didn't know each other well and they went their separate ways after graduation.

They both landed good jobs. Don went to work for a large computer hardware company, while Wendy started at a smaller software development firm. They each scored a $10,000 signing bonus and a $75,000 starting salary. The benefits were rich, too, with each company offering health insurance, paid time off, and matching contributions in a 401(k) retirement plan. As if that weren't enough, they also had no student loans or other debt. They had their entire lives in front of them.

It's here that their stories diverge.

The Ride

Don used his signing bonus as a down payment on a brand new 5 Series BMW. He knew it was a splurge, but he had earned it. After four years of sacrifice in school, he was due. Besides, on his salary, he could easily afford the $500 monthly payments. The salesperson at the dealership helped him make the calculations and assured him that he could afford the car. Salespeople are nice that way.

Don was happy.

Wendy rewarded herself, too. She took the $10,000 bonus and invested it in a low-cost index mutual fund. It felt good to know that through her hard work she was able to begin building wealth for her future. She was proud, in a good way, of what she had accomplished, and this investment was a constant reminder of both her past accomplishments and her future goals. As for a car, she continued to drive the beater with 100,000 miles on it that she had used in college.

Wendy was happy.

The Apartment

Don moved into a very nice apartment about 20 miles from work. He considered living closer to work but he could get a nicer place for the money further from the city. Besides, he reasoned, the commute wouldn't be so bad in the Beemer. Like the car, the apartment was a splurge; the rent was $1,500 a month. But Don was confident he could make the payment easily, given his salary. He was also confident that his salary would be going up significantly over time.

Don was really happy with his choices.

Wendy moved close enough to work so she could walk. She shared a three-bedroom apartment with two roommates, and her share of the rent was $700 a month. While the rent was more than she wanted to spend, she saved on car insurance, repairs, and gas because she was able to walk to work each day. In fact, she figured she wouldn't need a new car for a long time. She also avoided the headache and wasted time of a long commute.

Wendy was really happy with her choices.

The Nest Egg

Don considered investing in his company's 401(k), but chose not to. With the cost of the BMW and the rent, he didn't have a lot of money left over. Besides, he reasoned, he was only 22 years old. He had plenty of time to save for retirement down the road, perhaps after he paid off his car loan.

He was still happy.

Wendy didn't think twice about investing in her 401(k). She immediately set up monthly contributions that enabled her to save the maximum amount. Her employer matched these contributions dollar for dollar up to 6% of her salary.

She was still happy.

Fast Forward 20 Years

Now let's fast forward 20 years. Let's assume that Wendy's decisions enable her to save 30% of her income each year (including the employer match). Don, on the other hand, doesn't save anything and goes into more and more debt. What do their financial lives look like two decades from now?

Don is easy to diagnose. He has no savings and mountains of debt. In this regard, he looks like the typical American. A blue pill. He lives a nice lifestyle. But he's like a hamster on a wheel, constantly hustling just to keep up with his financial obligations.

Wendy is a different story. By saving 30% of her $75,000 salary, she's built up quite a nest egg. Assuming a 9.3% nominal return on her investments, Wendy has accumulated more than $1.3 million. And that's assuming no pay raises and no increase in her savings.

The point is not to admire the more than $1 million that Wendy has accumulated. The point is that Wendy is in control of her future. Don's future is dictated for him by the financial decisions he's made. That's not to say that Don can't turn things around. He can. But he has a lot of work and some difficult decisions ahead of him.

In contrast, Wendy can pursue whatever life purpose inspires her. If that means continuing to work at her small software company, she can do so without financial worry. Or she can start her own business, or move to a different job, or take a sabbatical.

Don and Wendy are fictional. The question you have to ask is whether you want to live like Don or like Wendy. This section of the book will show you how to live like Wendy. The ultimate choice is up to you.

CHAPTER 14

Freedom First, Lattes Second

"Do not save what is left after spending, but spend what is left after saving."
– Warren Buffett

I have friends who are natural born savers. They hate spending money. They order water when we go out to eat and often share a meal with each other. They change the oil in their car. They find deals on everything.

If that's you, saving money is a breeze. It's part of your DNA. Heck, you can probably skip this section of the book.

For the rest of us, it's not so easy.

I've learned one very important lesson about money over the past three decades. Relying on willpower alone to save money rarely works. Willpower may get the job done for a time, but eventually we let our guard down.

It's just like dieting. By sheer force of will, we may be able to lose a few pounds. But as the pounds come off, our willpower subsides. And eventually it's all ice cream and fries. They call it a yo-yo diet, and you can end up weighing more than when you started.

The same thing can happen with money.

Some event in our life motivates us to finally buckle down and take control of our money. Maybe it's an unexpected medical bill. Or perhaps our car bites the dust and we're faced with the expense of buying a new one. Whatever it is, it motivates us to get our financial house in order.

And we do it for a time. We create a budget, get serious about paying down debt, and maybe even save a little. And then our motivation subsides a bit, and things start to go downhill. In extreme cases, we can end up with more debt than what we started with.

It's called yo-yo debt. It's a thing.

NerdWallet shares the story of Chris Browning. He started out with $5,000 in debt. He got serious about his finances, started budgeting, and paid off his debt. Six months later, however, he and his new wife were struggling with $14,000 in credit card debt, mostly from their wedding. Two years later their debt had grown to $27,000.

As Chris explained, "Between finding a new place to live, school costs, medical bills, and just poor decisions, our debt grew to just under $27,000 by November of 2014."[18]

How do we prevent this from happening to us? We create the right environment and systems so that we don't have to rely exclusively on willpower. Think of it like getting all the junk food out of your house and having a chef prepare healthy meals for you.

It's a simple three-step process.

1. Save First

I've created countless budgets. Each time I'd use a piece of paper or a spreadsheet to write out all of my expenses. The fixed expenses were easy, like the mortgage payment and car insurance. The variable expenses got a little trickier, like utilities, groceries, and entertainment. The toughest categories were the periodic expenses, like gifts and vacations.

Then I'd add it all up and check out how much we had left at the end of the month.

Wrong. Wrong. Wrong.

Save first. Spend second.

Before you allocate a nickel of your income to expenses, decide first how much you'll *save*. This process may require a glimpse into your expense cate-

---

18 https://www.nerdwallet.com/blog/finance/yo-yo-debtors/

gories, particularly those expenses that are true necessities. But arrive at your Saving Rate first, and then spend the rest.

Some may argue that this is just a gimmick. At the end of the day, you have "x" amount of money and expenses have to be paid. They are right, in a way. "Save first, spend second" *is* a mindset. But it's the *right* mindset.

It tells you that *saving* is the priority. Freedom first, lattes second. It's also liberating. Once you've set aside what you'll save from each paycheck, you have the freedom to spend everything that's left.

There's also some science behind the Save First Philosophy. Beginning in 2006, companies with a 401(k) or other retirement plan could automatically enroll new employees into the plan.[19] That's right. Without the employee signing up, the employer could take money out of their paycheck and deposit it into the employee's 401(k) account.

The idea was to encourage employees to save for retirement. At first glance, this looks like a gimmick. Keep in mind...

- It only takes a few minutes for you to sign up for your employer's retirement plan; AND
- If the employer signs you up, you can cancel the program at any time, and it only takes a few minutes.

Given the above, this gimmick couldn't possible work, right? But it did.

Studies have shown that companies that use auto-enrollment have a higher percentage of employees who contribute to their 401(k), AND the employees on average contribute more money.[20]

How can this be?

It's simple. Out of sight, out of mind. The money comes out of an employee's

---

19 Companies could auto-enroll employees into workplace retirement accounts before 2006. But the Pension Protection Act of 2006 provided a "safe-harbor" that made the practice more commonplace. This is probably more than you want or need to know, but if you are interested in the backstory, check out http://www.pensionrights.org/issues/legislation/automatic-enrollment-401ks

20 https://institutional.vanguard.com/iam/pdf/CIRAE.pdf. It also helps when employers automatically increase the percentage withheld each year. https://www.pionline.com/article/20170626/ONLINE/170629886/contribution-gap-for-auto-enrollment-narrows-record-keepers-report

paycheck immediately. They never see the money in their checking account. They never have a chance to spend it. It takes our emotional attachment to money out of the equation.

The process is also automated. The 401(k) contribution is automatically deducted from a paycheck and deposited into the retirement plan. That brings us to Step #2.

2. Automate

Once you decide on your Saving Rate, automate the process. You want the money you'll save to be removed automatically from your checking account as soon as you get paid.

This happens automatically with a 401(k) or other employer-sponsored retirement account. You never see the money. It doesn't even land in your checking account. Your employer takes it from your pay and deposits it for you into your retirement account.

We need to do the same with other amounts we save. You can have your employer direct deposit your pay into more than one account. Have your savings sent over to a savings or investment account and your spending money into your checking account.

If your employer doesn't offer direct deposit, set up the automatic transfers with your bank. You can have a set amount transferred to a savings account and a set amount transferred to an investment account. And that's true even if these accounts are at different financial institutions—which brings us to our third step.

> **Resource**: A number of companies have introduced apps to help automate your savings. Perhaps you've heard of some of them. *Acorns* and *Stash* are two of the more popular options. Because companies are introducing new apps all the time, I've put together a resource that lists the current options, and I'll be updating the list regularly. You can check it out here: www.retirebeforemomanddad. com/resources.

3. Separate

We want to make the money we save as difficult as possible to access. For this reason, set up a savings account at an online bank that is not the one where you keep your checking account. I use Ally Bank, but there are many great options.[21]

There are two advantages to doing this. First, you'll likely earn a higher interest rate on your savings. Online banks typically pay more in interest than traditional brick and mortar banks. Second, it's a bit harder to access your money. You can't walk into a bank branch to take out your money. And if you don't get a debit card, you can't use an ATM either. You have to initiate an online transfer, which takes several days.

Think of this as keeping the junk food out of your house.

For investments, you can do the same thing. Set up an account at Vanguard, for example, and have a set amount transferred automatically to your account.

Here you may have several questions:

- How do I decide how much to move to a savings account versus an investment account?
- Heck, how do I set up an investment account?
- And once set up, what do I invest in?

All great questions and we'll get to them in the next section of the book.

Before we move on, however, it's important to understand that you'll follow the above steps more than once. You'll follow them when you first decide how much to save; and you'll follow them as you change your spending habits. Keep that in mind as we move to what I call The Money Audit.

---

21 https://www.doughroller.net/banking/high-yield-online-savings-account/

3 KEY TAKEAWAYS

1. Save first, and then spend what's left.

2. Automate your savings; don't rely on your willpower.

3. Separate your Freedom Fund from your primary checking account.

Take Action: Automate your savings. Set up a direct deposit of the amount you plan to save so it goes to an online savings account or other investment account. If that's not an option, set up automatic transfers with your bank. If you use transfers, schedule them to occur as soon as you get paid.

CHAPTER 15

The Money Audit

"You have a choice! You can throw in the towel,
or you can use it to wipe the sweat off your face!"

– Anonymous

Most people equate saving money with sacrifice. It feels like a sacrifice to eat out less, buy fewer clothes, take fewer or less expensive vacations, go without 500 cable channels. And we don't like sacrifice.

Early in my days of blogging, I wrote an article entitled "Painless Ways to Save Money."[22] The idea was to come up with a long list of ways to reduce our expenses without making significant changes to our lifestyle.

An example of this is car insurance. If you have a car, you have car insurance. It's a fact of life. But what if you could find the same car insurance somewhere else for less? It would entail no changes to your lifestyle, and it would reduce your expenses. And if you can save $5 a week with a little comparison shopping, you could turn that savings into $4,285 in ten years (The Rule of 857 x $5).

As I thought about these painless ways to save money, the idea of what I call the *One-N-Done* system to saving money came to light. In our car insurance example, we are able to save money month after month by taking the one simple step of comparing auto rates. Compare that to saving money by eating out less. That's a perfectly fine way to save money, but it requires constant effort. You only save money so long as you continue not to eat out. The same is true

---

22 https://www.doughroller.net/smart-spending/51-painless-money-saving-tips/

with clipping coupons. It's a great way to save money, but stop clipping and you stop saving.

The ideas of "Painless Ways to Save Money" and the *One-N-Done* System came together to form **The Money Audit**. Here's how it works.

Step #1: Write down every monthly bill you have, including the amount.

So much of our money is spent without thought. This is particularly true for those who automate their finances. Everything from the mortgage to utilities to cable is paid automatically from our bank account or charged to a credit card. The goal of this first step is to make a complete list of all of these monthly expenses.

Here is a list of common monthly bills:

- Rent or mortgage
- Credit card debt
- Car loans
- School loans
- All other debt
- Utilities (electric, gas, water, trash service)
- Internet, cable, home phone, and cell phone
- Netflix, YouTube TV, Hulu, Amazon Prime, and other subscription-based services
- Insurance (car, life, health, homeowners)

For each item, include the amount of the monthly expense. If the expense varies, as with utilities, you can record an average. A guesstimate is fine too, if you don't track your expenses each month. For loans, include the minimum monthly payment and the interest rate.

Creating a complete list is critical. Miss an item and you may miss an opportunity to save. To make sure you haven't missed anything, check your credit card and bank statements. Trust me, it's likely that you forgot something. Remember: out of sight, out of mind.

Step #2: Once you have a complete list, ask the following three questions for every item on the list:

Question 1: Do I really need or want this?

If the answer is "no," get rid of it and move to the next item. If the answer is yes, move to question #2. It's easy to blow by this question and move on. I encourage you to give some real thought to this question for every item on your list. At this stage, we so often make snap decisions.

Here's a hypothetical but very realistic conversation around question #1:

"Of course I need a car. How else would I get to work?" she said.

"Perhaps, but what would happen if you didn't have a car?" I replied.

"I'd die," she said.

"No seriously. What. Would. You. Do?" I replied.

And it's here that folks I talk to start to give serious thought to the question. It doesn't mean everybody sells their car, of course. I have a car. But it forces us out of our preconceived ideas of how we "must" live our lives.

We'll be exploring these ideas in the next two chapters. For now, carefully examine every item on your list and imagine what your life would be like without each item.

Question 2: Do I need exactly what I have?

For those items you've decided to keep in your life, can you change them in some way and save money? A perfect example is increasing the deductible on your car insurance. If you have an emergency fund that can cover a higher deductible, this simple change can save you hundreds of dollars a year.

While every situation is different, here are some common ways that many of us can save money in Step #2 of The Money Audit:

- Increase insurance deductibles.
- Decrease the amount of life insurance (if you are over insured, as many are).
- Move to a lower-cost cell phone provider (e.g., Cricket or Republic Wireless).
- Move to a lower-tier cable package.
- Reduce your internet speed.
- Refinance debt to a lower interest rate.

- Get a roommate.
- Pay your car insurance premium for six months instead of one month at a time.

Running doughroller.net for more than a decade enabled me to meet some incredible people. One of them was Abby Hayes. Abby worked with me for years as a writer and editor, and she continues to write for the site today. One topic she has covered is Airbnb. She and her husband rent out a room in their home. The income has grown to the point where it covers their mortgage.

I get that not everybody wants to rent out a room in their home. Abby's story, however, is a reminder of the creative ways people can make the most of their money. You can read more about Abby and Airbnb here: https://www.retirebeforemomanddad.com/AbbyHayes.

Question 3: Can I get what I need for less?

The simple act of comparison shopping once a year can save you a bundle. Comparison shop for EVERYTHING. At least once a year, check out prices for alternatives on everything from insurance to cable to trash service. A few simple phone calls can save significant money. And in some cases, your current providers may be willing to lower the price to keep you as a customer.

Here, a special note about debt is in order. The two best ways to get out of debt fast are to (1) sell the item that got you into debt (e.g., selling a car that you shouldn't have purchased in the first place), or (2) refinance debt to a lower interest rate. We'll cover debt in more detail later in the book.

Step #3: Execute. Once you have your list and know how you can save money, it's time to make the changes. This often involves a lot of phone calls.

How much you can save will, of course, depend on your specific circumstances and life goals. Using the Rules of 857 and 36,036, we know the following:

- Every $100 saved and invested each month will turn into $21,425 in 10 years ($25 x 857).

- Every $100 saved and invested each month will turn into $900,900 in 45 years ($25 x 36,036).

Don't forget too that for every $100 a month you reduce your expenses, you reduce your Level 7 Freedom Fund goal by $30,000. Let's take a second to make sure you know how I got that number. We reduce our expenses by $100 a month. This savings equals $1,200 a year. Level 7 Financial Freedom means having 25 years of expenses in the bank. So, $1,200 multiplied by 25 equals $30,000.

And keep in mind that these savings come from moves that (1) don't involve significant changes to your lifestyle, and (2) involve modest effort just one time. Let me give you an example from my own life.

Confession time. We had cable TV. Specifically, we had Verizon FIOS for cable, internet, and telephone service. We recently got rid of our $100 a month cable package (we kept internet and phone service) and replaced it with $35 a month YouTube TV.

We get all the channels we want. We no longer have to rent a DVR. *YouTube TV* comes with the ability to record shows. And we can watch TV from any device, including our iPhones and iPad. Most days, I use my iPhone to listen to business news while biking to the gym.

Total Monthly Savings: $65.

The Federal Communications Commission (FCC) publishes an annual report on cable service. According to its most recent report (2015), the average cost of basic cable is $22.63 a month. The average cost of expanded basic cable is $64.41. These prices hardly seem extreme. Just about everybody could afford either basic or expanded basic cable at these prices. Why? Because all we see is the monthly price. We don't see what these small numbers could mean over a decade of time or longer.

So let's open our eyes.

My $65 a month in savings will grow into a pile of cash. Here are the numbers, all assuming a 9.3% return:

10 Years: $12,794.00
20 Years: $45,104.47
30 Years: $126,702.56

And all of this comes from a simple, one-time change that doesn't affect our lifestyle at all. In fact, one could argue that it has improved our lives, because *YouTube TV* is far better than traditional cable. At least it is for us.

Before we move on, there's one more critical point to cover. Let's assume you apply The Money Audit to your own spending. You reduce your cable bill, car insurance, and cell phone bill, thus saving $150 a month. Great.

Now automate it.

From the last chapter, you are saving first, automating your savings, and separating your savings—away from easy reach. Take the money you've saved and increase your automated savings by that amount.

Fail to do this, and you'll likely spend the money on something else. Worse, you'll have no idea where it went. Increase your automated savings and you know exactly where it went—to buying your Financial Freedom.

We've covered The Money Audit in our free weekly newsletter (http://www.doughroller.net/newsletter). In 2013, I received a ton of emails from newsletter subscribers sharing with me just how much they saved. For some it was $50 a month, and for many it was hundreds or even thousands of dollars each month.

More recently, I asked the Dough Roller Facebook group (http://www.doughroller.net/facebookgroup) what steps they took to save money. Here are some of their responses (some responses have been edited for clarity):

> **David S.**: "Switched cell phone providers to Mint. Saves us $500 a year. Negotiated internet price every year. Saving $30 a month over regular pricing. LED light bulbs lowered monthly usage. Shopping at Aldi's saves us easily $30 a trip."

> **Roger B.**: "Changed cell service to another carrier and saved $134/month ($1,600/year)."

> **Claire M.**: "Moved into a studio instead of a high-rise two-bed, saved $150/mo. Bike to work/around town as much as

possible rather than using the paid off car: hard to quantify but in terms of gas and maintenance $40/mo. Will go up to $300/month after I get rid of the car and get a full bus pass."

Sebastian B.: "Threatened to cancel cable, internet, and home phone services with Spectrum. Reduced bill from $200 to $120 for next 12 months."

Nicole S.: "Switch[ed] car insurance companies, and paid six months upfront vs. month to month."

David D.: "Change[d] car and home insurance and saved $1,000 a year!"

Chris Q.: "I've cancelled my gym membership and bought multiple sets of dumbbells, an exercise ball, resistance bands, a medicine ball, etc., and I do everything on my own at home. It saves me $65 a month."

Tyler J.: "Cancelled cable, only use Netflix and Hulu ($103 savings/month). Switched from Verizon to AT&T FirstNet plan for first responders ($26 savings/month). Cancelled second gym membership ($20 savings/month). Designated a once a week "swipe night," so I now allow myself to swipe my card for eating out only once a week. ($200+ savings/month... yes, I was eating out a lot). Bought a French press and make my coffee at home, and I buy bulk coffee at BJs/Sams Club ($70-80 savings/month)."

Andrea S.: "We got SimpliSafe, and it costs us $180/year ($15/month). It saves us $270/year on our homeowner's insurance. We bought a refurbished SimpliSafe alarm system for $200 about five years ago."

David G.: "Shopped our house and auto insurance, which resulted in savings of $3000 a year. Included in new rates was umbrella insurance. Then we switched TV providers from

Dish Network to DirecTV Now streaming service, saving us
$65 a month. We shopped our cell phone plan and found
additional savings of $50. Been a good year—it just required
due diligence on our part."

The list goes on. And notice that the majority of these savings: (1) required
little, if any, change in lifestyle, and (2) required just one action that resulted in
savings month after month.

You can also save money by changing your lifestyle. We'll return to this idea
in the next two chapters. Before we move on, however, there's one more critical
thing to cover.

The One-N-Done System can *Make* You Money, Too

The One-N-Done System is about painless ways to save money. But there are
also painless ways to *make* money.

Imagine making hundreds of dollars a month in extra income without
working more or changing your lifestyle in any way. Here are two examples.

Cash Back Credit Cards

In the personal finance world, credit cards get a bad rap. I think Dave Ramsey
is partly the cause as he believes that one should never, ever, under any circumstances, use a credit card. I'm not here to push anybody to credit cards. They do
cause a lot of pain. Well, irresponsible use of credit cards causes the pain, but
I'm splitting hairs.

For those who control their spending and pay off their cards in full every
month, cash back cards can add a not insignificant boost to your Freedom
Fund. Will rewards credit cards by themselves make you rich? Of course not.
But they can add to your wealth and speed up your journey to Level 7.

Let me give you an example:

My wife and I use the Citi Double Cash credit card for virtually everything. It pays 2% cash back on all purchases (technically, 1% when you make the purchase and 1% when you pay the credit card bill).

Let's assume a family spends $5,000 a month and can charge half of these expenses to a credit card. Using a 2% cash back card will generate $50 a month. And we know what that means:

- Every $50 saved and invested each month will turn into $10,712.50 in 10 years ($12.50 a week x 857).
- Every $50 saved and invested each month will turn into $450,450 in 45 years ($12.50 a week x 36,036).

We don't get the Slingshot Effect because using a cash back card doesn't lower our expenses. But it does offer "free" money we can add to our Freedom Fund every month.

401(k) Match

The 401(k) match is where we really make some dough. Some companies match employee contributions to 401(k), 403(b), and other workplace retirement plans. The rules of these matching contributions vary from one employer to the next. Some match 50 cents for every dollar an employee contributes. Some match dollar for dollar. All have matching contribution limits, typically 6% of your income.

Let's see how this would work with our hypothetical $75,000 a year earner. Six percent of that income is $4,500. If we contribute at least that amount to the retirement plan, some employers will match 50 cents on the dollar ($2,250), while others will match dollar for dollar ($4,500).

Over a traditional 45-year working career, these matching contributions add up to a large pile of cash:

- $2,250 for 45 years at a 9.3% return: $1,539,729.05
- $4,500 for 45 years at a 9.3% return: $3,079,458.10

And that's just from the company match. The numbers don't factor in *your* contributions.

Now, recall that it would take about 31 years to reach Level 7 Financial Freedom based on a 20% Saving Rate. Using our previous example:

- Annual Income: $75,000
- Saving Rate: 20% ($15,000 a year)
- Spending Rate: 80% ($60,000 a year)

We would speed up our journey to Level 7 Financial Freedom with an employer match:

- A $2,250 annual match reduces our Level 7 journey from about 31 years to less than 30 years.
- A $4,500 annual match reduces our Level 7 journey from about 31 years to about 28 years.

If your employer matches retirement contributions: Take. Advantage. Of. The. Match.

3 KEY CONCEPTS

1. The best ways to save money are painless and require action just once.

2. These principles, Painless Ways to Save Money and One-N-Done, come together in The Money Audit.

3. Conduct a Money Audit at least once a year.

Take Action: Conduct your own Money Audit. Be sure to automate any money saved so that it goes toward your Financial Freedom. Then join the Facebook group and let us know the amount of monthly savings you achieved.

CHAPTER 16

The Power of Habit

"We are what we repeatedly do. Excellence, then, is not an act, but a habit."
— Will Durant

Recently, I had lunch with a former law partner of mine. He's an attorney who has done very well for himself, building a net worth of about $5 million by his mid-fifties. Did he want to discuss the latest stock tip or investing strategy? Nope. Here's what he wanted to know…

Is it better to focus on the small, everyday expenditures or the big-ticket items?

My answer was simple—yes. In the last chapter we looked at recurring monthly bills. Using The Money Audit, you learned how to evaluate each and every monthly bill and either get rid of it or reduce its cost.

Now let's turn to what I call Lifestyle Expenses. Here we are talking about everything from a daily latte to an annual vacation. It's here that we are going to take an unusual approach.

First, here's what I'm NOT going to do:

- Demand you never drink another latte (I'm sipping one as I type these words).
- Insist that you scrap that vacation you have planned to the Galapagos Islands.
- Try to convince you to get rid of Netflix, Hulu, YouTube TV, Sling TV, and Amazon Prime.

Instead, I want to introduce you to two powerful and related concepts—the Myth of Sacrifice and the Power of Habit.

The Myth of Sacrifice

David Bach published *The Automatic Millionaire: A Powerful One-Step Plan to Live and Finish Rich* in 2005. In his book he introduced the concept of the Latte Factor. As you know, if we can save small amounts of money each day, money we might otherwise spend on a latte, for example, we can accumulate a sizable amount of wealth.

It seems simple enough to me. We've already looked at the power of small investments. Yet David's Latte Factor generated a lot of backlash.

Some argued with the numbers. Helaine Olen, author of *Pound Foolish: Exposing the Dark Side of the Personal Finance Industry*, took issue with a latte costing $5 and Bach's assumption of a 10 or 11 percent return.[23]

She raises some important points. A 10 or 11 percent return assumption, as we now know, is huge. Even the difference between 10 and 11 percent is big. It may not seem like a big difference, but over time, the difference between a 10 percent and 11% return is like the difference between a lightning bolt and a lightning bug. They may sound similar at first, but they ain't.

Yet there's still a lot to learn from the Latte Factor. As David Bach explains:

"The Latte Factor is a METAPHOR for how we waste small amounts of money on small things. It's a teaching method to get people to "rethink" how they spend money and realize they have more than enough to start saving. It's not about guaranteed returns, and my books don't promise 10 percent returns. And my books show in many cases compounded interest rate examples from 1 percent to 10 percent."

The more interesting criticism has to do with lifestyle. Should we really give up a morning latte we enjoy so that we can retire comfortably 45 years from now? Even an early retirement 20 or 25 years from now is a long time to go

---

23 https://www.businessinsider.com/pound-foolish-the-latte-factor-isnt-true-helaine-
    olen-2012-12

without a latte. That doesn't sound very appealing.

Not long ago I would go to a coffee shop nearly every single day and order a mocha. I love chocolate. And I loved the environment at coffee shops. I would take my laptop and pretend I was one of the cool kids. Yes, I embarrass my children. That's what dads do. It's in our DNA.

Then one day I just stopped. Not embarrassing my children; that will never stop. I stopped getting a mocha every day. In fact, I went cold turkey.

In my case, I stopped more for health reasons than financial reasons. But I stopped. It was painful at first. I couldn't get mocha lattes out of my mind. It was all I thought about.

And talk about sacrifice. It hurt.

But then it didn't. It took a couple of weeks to adjust. And then I didn't miss the mocha. I didn't even want one. I haven't had a mocha in years. And it's no sacrifice at all. In fact, I'm happier today without my daily mocha than I was when I thought I needed it to make life worth living. Funny how our minds play tricks on us.

This experience took me back to a similar event in my childhood. When I was a teenager, my mom and stepdad were in financial trouble. The combination of a failed business and a terrible economy caused us to almost lose our home. We didn't, but money was tight.

And then the unthinkable happened—our TV broke. This was in the early 1980s when most families had just one TV. I know, I'm old.

Because we had no money, we couldn't get the TV repaired. And we certainly couldn't afford to buy a new one. Oh, the horrors. I can still remember coming home from school and for a split second forgetting that the TV didn't work. As I had done for years, I automatically headed for the family room, only to remember that the TV was nothing but a large paper weight. Sacrifice doesn't begin to explain the feeling of loss I suffered.

But a funny thing happened after a couple of weeks. I slowly forgot about the TV. It was no longer an option, so I moved on. After about a month, the lack of a TV was not a sacrifice. It just became part of our reality, and so we passed the time in other ways.

And so it is with many of the things we buy.

In the end, the Latte Factor isn't about avoiding things that bring us plea-sure. It's about making sure that how we spend our money truly brings us the joy in life that we desire. In many cases, we spend money out of habit, and the happiness is fleeting.

The Power of Habit

The mocha lesson brings us to the second important concept of this chapter—the Power of Habit. So much of what we do is out of habit. We have a morning routine that's now a strongly embedded habit. We drive to work the same way without giving it much thought—habit. We buy our lunch at work every day—habit. We go out to dinner two or three times a week—habit.

Think about your daily and weekly routines. We have routines at home and at work. If you are a coffee drinker, you probably drink about the same amount of coffee at about the same times every day. The same is true if you are a smoker.

Not all habits are bad, of course. And habits are important. If we had to think through every little decision we made each day, we'd go mad. Imagine having to think through how to brush your teeth step-by-step every morning.

Habits can also be destructive or at least suboptimal. Our beliefs that we need certain things to be happy lock us into routines that are very hard to break. Add to that our failure to realize that many of our decisions are born from habits, and change becomes very difficult. However, once you break just one routine and realize that it didn't bring you the happiness you thought it did, you begin to take back your own life. You begin to live intentionally. And this "small" win empowers you to take back control in other areas of your life.

In his bestselling book, *The Power of Habit*, Charles Duhigg discusses what he calls *keystone habits*. These are habits that, once developed, help us form good habits in other areas of our lives. One keystone habit is regular exercise. Developing the habit of weekly exercise can help us in other areas of our lives, including our finances. As Duhigg explains:

"When people start habitually exercising, even as infrequently as once a week, they start changing other, unrelated patterns in their lives, often unknowingly. Typically, people who exercise start eating better and becoming more productive at work. They smoke less and show more patience with colleagues and family. They use their credit cards less frequently and say they feel less stressed. It's not completely clear why. But for many people, exercise is a keystone habit that triggers widespread change."

We can learn two important lessons here. First, there may be a connection between exercise and credit card use. No judgment here, but maybe we should all start exercising. Second, exercising as little as once a week can produce positive results in multiple areas of our lives.

In turns out that small wins can produce big results (not unlike the Money Multiplier). From Duhigg's book:

> "Small wins are exactly what they sound like, and are part of how keystone habits create widespread changes. A huge body of research has shown that small wins have enormous power, an influence disproportionate to the accomplishments of the victories themselves. 'Small wins are a steady application of a small advantage,' one Cornell professor wrote in 1984. 'Once a small win has been accomplished, forces are set in motion that favor another small win.' Small wins fuel transformative changes by leveraging tiny advantages into patterns that convince people that bigger achievements are within reach."

How do we now apply the Myth of Sacrifice and the Power of Habit to our financial lives?

Step #1: Identify Your Financial Habits

The first step is to think about how you routinely spend money. Here it may be helpful to track everything you spend for two weeks. If you use a credit or debit card for most purchases, you can review your most recent statements.

From this information, look for patterns in your spending. Perhaps you go out to lunch at work every day. Or perhaps you have a habit of signing up for various subscription services (news, entertainment, productivity tools) that over time you stop using. Or it could be that you have a habit of regularly buying "stuff" (gadgets, clothes, crap from Walmart). For some the issue is not what but when. Perhaps your spending occurs on the weekend because you need something to do.

The point is to take 30 minutes and examine your financial life to identify spending patterns and routines.

Step #2: Pick One Spending Habit to Change

You may identify any number of spending habits that need to change. Here, however, we want to pick just *one* to start with. Limiting this step to just one habit is critical. If you try to change too much at once, you are more likely to fall short of your goal. It's like deciding all at once that you'll never again eat sugar, salt, bread, fried foods, and processed food. Good goals, perhaps, but a lot to tackle at one time. Pick one habit you want to change.

Step #3: Replace the Habit with a Better Habit

Once you identify the habit or routine you want to change, replace it with something positive. Rather than just cancelling your weekly night out on the town that would cost you a lot of money, replace it with something fun to do that costs less. Rather than just cutting back on eating out, replace it with an extra special meal at home. Rather than just shopping until you drop when you are feeling depressed, ride your bike or go for a walk with a friend.

In *The Power of Habit*, Duhigg calls replacing bad routines with good ones— *The Golden Rule of Habit Change*. He describes a habit loop that involves a Cue, a Routine, and Rewards.

As an example, you may eat out at lunchtime every day. For you, the Cue may be *time*. You go to lunch every day at noon. The Routine may be that you leave your office building and go to a nearby restaurant or food court. Now what's the Reward? The obvious answer is food, of course. However, perhaps the real reward is getting out of the office.

Here we want to replace the routine itself. Rather than going out to lunch, you bring your lunch but still leave the office to eat it. Perhaps you go to a nearby park or coffee shop. The key is to replace a current routine you want to change with a new, more positive one.

As Duhigg explains: "Attempts to give up smoking, for instance, will often fail unless there's a new routine to satisfy old cues and reward urges. A smoker usually can't quit unless she finds some activity to replace cigarettes when her nicotine craving is triggered."

Step #4: Automate Your Savings

This last step is critical. Take the money you'll save from changing your routine and add it to your automated savings. This could mean increasing your 401(k) contribution. It could mean increasing what you transfer to a savings account. It could mean increasing what you transfer to an investment account. It could also mean increasing how much you are paying on your debt. If you don't do this, you'll end up spending the money on something else. And you may not even remember what you spent it on.

The Latte Factor Revisited

So the point of the Latte Factor is not that you should avoid Starbucks every day. I'm certainly not here to tell you that. Rather, the Latte Factor can teach us three important lessons:

1. Small amounts of money, invested over time, turn into large amounts of wealth.

2. What at first seems like a sacrifice may in time not be a sacrifice at all. The only way to know is to make a change for 21 days (more about this in the next chapter).

3. We spend money out of habit. Whether it's a latte, lunch at work, or the Hulu Plus subscription we completely forgot about, habits and routines can drive a lot of our financial decisions. Every now and again we should revisit those habits to make sure they are aligned with our priorities and what truly makes us happy.

3 KEY CONCEPTS

1. We spend money and live our lives out of habit, and some of our habits have been developed over many years.

2. Changing our habits will be painful at first.

3. Over time, however, we may find that changes that at first seemed like a sacrifice actually saved us money and made our lives more enjoyable.

CHAPTER 17

What if?

"All life is an experiment. The more experiments you make the better."
– Ralph Waldo Emerson

I love the game of chess—but not the occasional game with a friend. I'm talking about tournament chess with clocks and everything. I have a library filled with chess books, chess playing software, online subscriptions to chess sites, and even chess databases. Chess can be devilishly deceiving. Some of the best moves in the game look like they should lose. But instead they win.

Imagine considering a pawn move when you suddenly realize your opponent could take your queen. As she is the most powerful piece on the board, you abandon the pawn move you were considering and you focus on how to save Her Majesty. You figure out a plan, save your queen, and all is right with the world.

After the game, win or lose, you enter the moves into a computer chess-playing program to evaluate the game. And to your shock and amazement, that pawn move would have been brilliant. Yes, your opponent could have won your queen. But it would have allowed you to checkmate your opponent and win the game.

If only you had continued your evaluation past the obstacle. If only you had considered the possibilities after losing your queen. Believe it or not, this happens a lot in chess. You look at a move and reject it because you think the result will be negative. That's sensible, right? But wait—not so fast.

I'd like to propose a thought experiment I call "What if."

In my chess example, it would go like this: What if I move my pawn? No, he'll take my queen. Okay, what if he takes my queen? Oh, I see it now. I have checkmate in three moves.

Let's apply this strategy to our money. Think about your life and the money you spend, and then ask yourself a series of "What if" questions. If you're like me, you'll start out small:

—What if I skipped my daily latte?
—What if I took my lunch to work?
—What if I ate out less?

As you ponder these things, you ratchet up the boldness in your "What if" questions:

—What if I scaled back my vacations?
—What if I got rid of cable TV?
—What if I biked to work a few times a week?

But even these questions are minor league. Here are the big-league questions:

—What if I got rid of one of my cars?
—What if I got rid of all of my cars?
—What if I downsized my home?
—What if I moved close enough to my job so that I could walk to work?
—If walking to work is impossible, what if I got a new job?
—What if I moved to a less expensive area of the country?

Some of these questions may raise an immediate objection. You think: I can't get rid of my car; that's impossible.

Take some time with these questions. Seriously. What would you do without a car? I'm guessing you'd survive. Your daily routine might change dramatically, but you'd survive. The point of this exercise is not to convince you to sell your car. *I* have one. Maybe you should have one too, or maybe not.

The point is to invoke our imagination. To think beyond our current situation. To consider what at first seems impossible. To dream.

Let's apply the "What if" test to owning a car.

What if I sell my car?

Most people immediately dismiss the idea: I can't sell my car; I need a car to get to work. How would I get to the grocery store, or the mall, or how would I run other errands? And that's where we stop thinking about it, stop questioning. We turn our brain off to the possibilities when we encounter the first obstacle.

It's here, however, that we need to push forward and ask "What if" again.

What if I sell my car and have to figure out a different way to get to work?

Just like a grandmaster in chess, we need to undertake some analysis. In this case, the analysis may go in several different directions:

—What if I take public transportation?
—What if I walk to work?
—What if I ride a bike to work?
—What if I carpool with a coworker or friend?
—What if I change jobs and work closer to home?
—What if I move and live closer to work?
—What if I find a job I can do from home?

These questions may in turn lead to more "What if" questions.

—What if I ask my boss if I can work from home a few days a week?
—What if I could work four 10-hour shifts?
—What if I use a combination of transportation methods, such as biking, carpooling, and Uber?

After all the analysis, you may very well decide not to sell your car. And sometimes you really do need to get your Queen out of harm's way. But sometimes, pressing into immediate objections with "What if" questions can reveal possibilities that you had never thought of before.

The 21-Day Experiment

Have you ever watched a game of chess where one player moves a piece but keeps his finger on it? He then looks around to see what he thinks of the move. If he doesn't like it, he returns the piece to its original square and looks for a different move.

In tournament chess, you can't do this. If you touch a piece, you must move it. It's called the "Touch Move" rule. And yes, tournament chess is serious business.

In life, however, we don't have to follow the Touch Move rule. We can move our pieces around, check things out, and put them back if we decide not to make that move.

How? By experimenting.

Write down the results of your "What if" questions. Make a list of those changes in your life that you would make if you could. Write them down even if they seem impossible.

Now run a 21-day experiment. Pick something on your list and try living without it for three weeks. For 21 days, decide to:

—Go without cable TV;
—Or eat out less;
—Or park one of your cars and not use it;
—Or skip Starbucks.

Not So Fun Fact: The average American spends about $1,100 a year on coffee. According to a survey conducted by Acorns, which is a savings app, 41% of millennials surveyed said they spent more on coffee last year than they saved for retirement.[24]

---

24 https://www.foxnews.com/food-drink/millennials-are-spending-more-money-on-coffee-than-retirement-plans

It's important that you focus on one change at a time. You'll likely find that the ideas on your "What if" list are about a lot more than money. They are about how you live your life. Trying to change too much at one time is a recipe for disaster, as we learned in the last chapter.

Remember to replace old habits with new ones. If you plan to go without cable TV for 21 days, find something to replace that activity. Don't just sit in your recliner staring at a blank TV screen. You may choose to read, play a game, or exercise. The key is to fill the void with something positive.

Many of the changes I've made have saved us money. Foregoing a mocha latte is one example. But the truth is I didn't do it for the money. In my case, it was to avoid the empty calories. But here's the key. What started out as a painful sacrifice turned into something that made me happier. I'm more content today because I don't go to a coffee shop every day and pound down a chocolate beverage.

We convince ourselves that saving money requires sacrifice. It may turn out, however, that the feeling of sacrifice fades over time. In fact, the change we made may make our lives more enjoyable. A series of 21-day experiments can help you figure out what truly makes you happy and deserves your hard-earned money.

Level 7

Before we leave this topic, let's take a quick look at how small changes in our habits can supercharge our journey to Level 7 Financial Freedom. We'll assume we earn $5,000 a month. We'll also assume that before making any changes, our Saving Rate is 10%.

With these assumptions, here's how much faster we will achieve Level 7 Financial Freedom based on changes we might make in our lives following a 21-day experiment. (Also, an estimate of the monthly savings is in parentheses.)

—Get rid of cable TV ($100): three years faster.
—Eating out less ($200): six years faster.
—Going without a car ($300): eight years faster.

And if you made all three changes, thus saving an extra $600 a month, you'd achieve Level 7 Financial Freedom more than a decade sooner. You'd reach Level 7 in about 30 years (at a 6.3% real return), rather than after nearly 43 years.

I use the above examples not because I believe you should get rid of cable TV, eat out less, or sell your car. We have to make these types of decisions for ourselves. These examples, however, teach us two important lessons:

1. We make decisions every day when we keep all these various things in our lives. They may have become habits that we give little thought to, but they are choices we are making. And we have the power to make changes if we want to.

2. These decisions have a significant effect on our financial lives.

3 KEY CONCEPTS

1. Our habits drive a lot of our behavior, including how we spend our money.

2. We've come to believe that certain things make us happy, when in fact they do not.

3. Running 21-day experiments is a simple way to test not only whether we can put more money toward our Freedom Fund, but also whether the way we are living today really makes us happy.

Take Action: Pick one financial experiment to run for 21 days.

CHAPTER 18

The #1 Freedom Fund Killer

"If you own a home with wheels on it and several cars without,
you just might be a redneck."

– Jeff Foxworthy

In the last chapter we imagined life without a car. I chose cars because they are the #1 Freedom Fund killer. My good friend Jeff Rose of GoodFinancialCents.com describes car payments as the #1 thing that's killing our wealth.[25] In this chapter I'm going to show you why.

The Average Cost of Owning a Car

How much do you think it costs to own a car? Of course the answer will vary, based on the type of car, cost of insurance, miles driven, and other factors.

According to the personal finance site, Nerd Wallet[26], here's a breakdown of the average cost of owning a new car:

$523	Car Payment
$98	Insurance
$146	Gas
$99	Maintenance & Repairs
$12	Registration, Fees & Taxes
$878	**Total**

---

25 https://www.forbes.com/sites/jrose/2018/10/02/the-one-monthly-payment-killing-your-wealth/#27a3b6b043c1

26 https://www.nerdwallet.com/blog/loans/total-cost-owning-car/

At this point, there can be no doubt about the kind of wealth we could build on $878 a month. Let's look at the numbers, again assuming a 9.3% annual return.

10 years	$172,817.43
20 years	$609,257.26
30 years	$1,711,459.25
40 years	$4,495,002.73

Now, before you send me hate mail, let me address some obvious issues:

First, not everybody can or wants to go without a car. I get it.

Second, even if you did go without a car, you wouldn't save $878 a month. You'd have to spend some amount of money on transportation.

Third, not everybody buys a new car. You may decide to buy a used car that costs a lot less than $523 a month.

Fourth, you may pay cash for a car. It's still money out the door that can't be invested but at least you're not paying interest.

Finally, the $523 average car payment doesn't last forever. Eventually you pay off the car and continue to drive it for some period of time.

All true. So let's dig a little deeper.

What If?

Let's compare two people who own cars. We'll assume one driver keeps her car longer than the other. Let's begin by establishing a baseline.

We'll assume that an individual, at age 25, pays $20,000 for a car. She pays cash, so we don't need to consider the interest payments. Five years later she sells the car for 50% of what she paid for it, and she buys another $20,000 car. She repeats this process until she buys her tenth car at age 70. We'll assume she sells her last car for $10,000 at age 75, and thereafter her children drive her where she needs to go (hint to my children).

We've left some things out. We've completely ignored inflation. That same car will cost a lot more 10, 20, or 30 years from now. We are also ignoring the cost of insurance, maintenance, repairs, fuel, interest on a car loan (if we don't pay cash), and Christmas tree fresheners to hang from the rearview mirror. The point is that the cost to *buy* a car is only the beginning.

But we'll keep things simple.

How much do these cars cost our fearless Freedom Fighter? At one level, the math is easy. The first car costs $20,000. Each car thereafter costs $10,000 ($20,000 less the proceeds from selling the previous car for $10,000). Add up the 10 purchases, and we arrive at $110,000.

But that's only half the picture. What if, instead of buying cars, she invested the money. How much would she have by the time she reached 75, assuming a 9.3% return?

Here's a breakdown of the results:

Car #1	$20,000 invested for 50 years (age 25 to 75)	$2,054,537.59 (That's one expensive car.)
Car #2	$10,000 invested for 45 years (age 30 to 75)	$646,421.34 (Amazing how just five years and $10,000 can change the result.)
Car #3	$10,000 invested for 40 years (age 35 to 75)	$406,768.46
Car #4	$10,000 invested for 35 years (age 40 to 75)	$255,963.99
Car #5	$10,000 invested for 30 years (age 45 to 75)	$161,068.44
Car #6	$10,000 invested for 25 years (age 50 to 75)	$101,354.27
Car #7	$10,000 invested for 20 years (age 55 to 75)	$63,778.40
Car #8	$10,000 invested for 15 years (age 60 to 75)	$40,133.33
Car #9	$10,000 invested for 10 years (age 65 to 75)	$25,254.39
Car #10	$10,000 invested for 5 years (age 70 to 75)	$15,891.63
Total Opportunity Cost Over a Lifetime of Car Purchases		**$3,771,171.84**

Are you sure you need a car? What if…?

Buying a car every five years under the assumptions outlined above will cost over $3.7 million in missed opportunities to build wealth over a lifetime. Now, imagine a couple buying *two* cars every five years.

You may be objecting to the idea of selling the car every five years. Good thinking. That tells me you are getting the hang of this. So let's compare the above with someone who drives each car for 10 years. We'll assume that at the end of each decade the car is worth just $5,000. How do the numbers stack up?

Car #1	$20,000 invested for 50 years (age 25 to 75)	$2,054,537.59 (That's still one expensive car.)
Car #2	$15,000 invested for 40 years (age 35 to 75)	$610,152.70
Car #3	$15,000 invested for 30 years (age 45 to 75)	$241,602.66
Car #4	$15,000 invested for 20 years (age 55 to 75)	$95,667.60
Car #5	$15,000 invested for 10 years (age 65 to 75)	$37,881.58
Total Opportunity Cost Over a Lifetime of Car Purchases		**$3,039,842.13**

Still a lot of money but a savings of more than $700,000. By driving the car longer, we add hundreds of thousands of dollars to our wealth. Of course, this assumes you **invest** what you aren't spending on the car.

Let's take it one step further. Let's assume our fearless Freedom Fighter drives each car 15 years, after which it has no resale value:

Car #1	$20,000 invested for 50 years (age 25 to 75)	$2,054,537.59
Car #2	$20,000 invested for 35 years (age 40 to 75)	$511,927.97
Car #3	$20,000 invested for 20 years (age 55 to 75)	$127,556.81
Car #4	$20,000 invested for 5 years (age 70 to 75)	$31,783.26
Total Opportunity Cost Over a Lifetime of Car Purchases		**$2,725,805.63**

Now we've saved more than $1 million. If you think driving the same car for 15 years is crazy, we just sold my wife's car that we bought 17 years ago. But again, this book isn't about me; it's about you.

One final set of numbers. So far, we've assumed the purchase of a $20,000 new car. Let's instead assume we buy a $15,000 car and drive it for 15 years before buying a new one.

Car #1	$15,000 invested for 50 years (age 25 to 75)	$1,540,903.19
Car #2	$15,000 invested for 35 years (age 40 to 75)	$383,945.98
Car #3	$15,000 invested for 20 years (age 55 to 75)	$95,667.60
Car #4	$15,000 invested for 5 years (age 70 to 75)	$23,837.44
Total Opportunity Cost Over a Lifetime of Car Purchases		**$2,044,354.21**

Now we've increased our savings to more than $1.7 million. Cars cost a fortune, and we haven't even dealt with insurance, gas and repairs.

Any way you can save on the cost of a car will go a long way to empowering your journey to Level 7. It may mean driving your car longer. It may mean buying a less expensive car (which also saves on insurance). It may mean a family that has one car instead of two. Or it may mean going without a car altogether.

Whatever you decide, I hope you now look at car ownership differently.

Let me leave you with a story about a guy named Ben. In April 2016, he was in an accident that totaled his car. He and his wife, April, decided to rent a car for a few months. They planned to buy a new car at the end of the summer. Like most people, they had lived their entire adult lives owning cars. And they were going to buy a new car.

Then they had the idea of maybe, just maybe, going *without* a car. They had gone down to one shared car a few years before. Yet the idea of not owning even one car seemed "un-American." But they decided to experiment. They would go without a car for a time and then buy a car when the experiment failed, as they assumed it would.

But the experiment was a success. Of course they had to make some changes. They walked and biked more, they took an Uber or Zipcar as necessary, and they even took the bus from time to time. It changed their shopping habits, particularly *where* they shopped (now closer to home), and it saved them a truckload (pun intended) of money.

As Ben explained, "Even with the Uber, taxi, and Zipcar bills, we saved money compared to owning a car. No more car insurance bills, parking lot charges, or campus parking fees. We were surprised at how much we had to

learn in order to go car-free: Alternate services, iPhone apps, Uber rules....
But we're proud of our accomplishment, and talking about it generates spirited
conversations about other environmentally friendly solutions. We know that
our location in Bethesda helps a lot, but we encourage others to find bold
solutions that work for them."[27]

27 https://www.washingtonpost.com/opinions/learning-to-love-life-without-a-
   car/2016/01/29/7ec1e34c-ba3e-11e5-b682-4bb4dd403c7d_story.html

3 KEY CONCEPTS

1. Cars are expensive.

2. Any way you can reduce your car expense can go a long way to super-charging your journey to Level 7.

3. Freedom first, cars second.

Part 4

Investing

The TV show *Lost* is about plane crash survivors on a deserted island. Think of it as a modern-day version of Gilligan's Island. In the show, the survivors discover an underground bunker manned by a guy named Desmond Hume. They learn from Hume that every 108 minutes he must enter a sequence of characters into a computer. If he fails to do so, the world as they know it will come to an end.

Beyond that, there's little that is known about "pressing the button," as Hume's action came to be known. Press the button every 108 minutes and life goes on. Fail to press the button on time and kaboom! Or maybe nothing happens.

As you might imagine, there was some disagreement over what to do. Some thought they should man the station and continue pressing the button. Others thought it was a hoax.

Because they didn't really know anything about this every 108-minute button thing, it was impossible to evaluate with any certainty the consequences of their decision. They didn't really know what they were doing and why, so they had no confidence that they were making the right decision. As you might expect, eventually they failed to press the button and...well, I won't spoil the show for you.

Investing is similar to pressing the button. It is incredibly easy. As you'll see in later chapters, you can create a well-diversified portfolio of stocks and bonds in about the time it takes to, well, press a button.

If you don't know why you are pressing the button, however, you'll have no confidence in what you are doing. You'll be like the *Lost* survivors debating what to do. During times when market values are falling, *and they will fall,* your lack of knowledge could cause you to make some serious mistakes. And when others challenge your approach to investing, *and it will happen*, you won't have a good response. It may cause you to question yourself. That's not a good place to be when it comes to your money and your future.

Freedom Fighters need to understand why they are doing what they are doing. The next few chapters will give you the foundation you need so you can press the button with confidence.

CHAPTER 19

Stocks & Bonds

"Jargon is the last refuge of the scoundrel."
– Roger Ebert

Over the next few chapters we'll cover key investing terms and concepts. At this point, don't worry about where you'll actually invest your money. We'll get to that soon enough. First, we need to build a solid foundation.

Investing terminology can be intimidating. Imagine you overhear somebody at work say, "My portfolio has been doing great. The tilt to emerging markets and small cap has really paid off. While I think equities are a little overvalued, the interest rate risk on bonds isn't any better."

Huh? It reminds me of the teacher in Charlie Brown, "Wah Wah, Wah Wah Wah Wahhhhh." Not to worry. This chapter and those that follow will help you translate things like "small cap."

The terms in this chapter are not meant to be memorized. There is no test at the end of the book. And life is an open book test anyway. You can always come back to this chapter to look up a term anytime you want. The key here is to demystify the language.

Let's get started in this chapter with two very important terms: **Stocks** and **Bonds**. (You'll find key terms in **bold** the first time they are introduced.)

Let's Start a Business

Let's imagine you and I start a business. A dry cleaning business perhaps. We each contribute $100,000 to the business in exchange for 50% ownership. Let's imagine our company issues 100 shares of **Stock**, which we divide between the two of us, 50-50. We quickly learn, however, that $200,000 is not enough money to start a dry cleaning business. Between the equipment, real estate, advertising, and other costs, we need more capital.

We have two options. First, we can sell some of our ownership in the business to an investor. Then we will no longer each own 50% of the business. If we sell 20% of our ownership, for example, we'd both be left owning 40%, and the investor would own the remaining 20%.

Selling equity to raise money has one big advantage—we don't have to pay it back. It isn't a loan; we are exchanging an ownership interest in our business for cash.

There are some downsides, however. First, we no longer each get 50% of the company's profits. We now get 40% each, with the investor pocketing 20%. And that's forever. Second, if we ever sell the business, 20% of the proceeds go to the investor. Still, selling some of our **Equity**, as it's called, in the business is one way to raise money. Equity and Stock generally refer to the same thing—ownership of a business.

Second, we could borrow the money. We could borrow from a bank or we could borrow from an investor. In this scenario, we don't give up any ownership in the business, so that's good news. We do, however, agree to pay interest on the amount of money we borrow. And we have a contractual obligation to repay the principal of the loan when it comes due.

Now let's look at this business from the investor's perspective. At first glance, lending the money seems safer than buying part of the company. In the world of investing, he would buy a **Bond** that represents the money he is lending to the dry cleaners. He would have a contract that requires the company to pay him interest and to return the money lent to the company when the bond **Matures**, that is, when the term of the bond comes to an end.

If the company fails to pay the interest when due, or the principal when the bond matures, we can file a lawsuit to recoup our money. Depending on the terms of the bond, we can even lay claim to the company's assets (remember all that equipment a dry cleaners needs in order to operate) to recover our money.

Bonds are not without risk. We've already identified one risk—the company fails to pay us. Yes, we can sue, but if things go really bad for the dry cleaners, they may not have the assets to pay us even if we win the lawsuit. This risk of not getting paid on our bond is called **Credit Risk**.

There's another risk more serious than the first. It's called **Interest Rate Risk**. Let's assume we agree to lend $100,000 to the dry cleaners for 10 years in exchange for annual interest payments of 7%. The dry cleaners makes interest payments every year and repays the principal of the loan after 10 years when the bond matures. At the time we made this deal, 7% was a competitive interest rate for similar bonds.

Now fast forward two years. Let's imagine interest rates have gone up. On a similar bond, investors are now getting 10% interest. Ouch. We are stuck with eight years left before the bond matures, and we are earning 3% less than the going rate for similar bonds. We could try to sell the bond, but who would buy it? Why would somebody buy our 7% bond when they could go invest in a new bond issued by another dry cleaners and earn 10%?

If we were really desperate to sell, we could sell the bond at a **Discount**. We could accept something less than the $100,000 face value of the bond. But how much less? Well, we could agree to enough of a discount so that the buyer could make up for the 3% difference between the interest on our 7% bond and the prevailing interest of 10% on new bonds. We could get rid of the bond but at a loss.

Unless we needed the money, we could hold the bond for the full 10-year term. We'd earn our 7% each year, and it might feel like we've avoided a loss, but we really haven't. We would still be missing out on the extra 3% that new bonds were paying.

Perhaps I shouldn't be so negative. Rather than interest rates rising, maybe they will go down. Two years from now the prevailing rates on 10-year bonds issued by dry cleaners might fall to 5%. In that case, our 7% bond looks fantastic. Heck, in a 5% interest rate environment, we'd love to lend money to dry cleaners at 7% forever.

And if we ever decided to sell the bond, we could sell it for a **Premium**. An investor would pay more than the $100,000 face value of our bond. How much more would we demand? Enough to make up the difference between our 7% bond and the current market rate of 5%.

Our dry cleaners example underscores an important aspect of bond investing. As interest rates rise, the value of existing bonds goes down. As interest rates fall, the value of existing bonds goes up.

As investors, we aren't limited to bonds. We could instead *buy* part of the dry cleaners. As noted above, we could buy 20% of the dry cleaners and share in the future profits of the company. How do we evaluate this potential investment?

Well, we'd first want to understand the future prospects of the dry cleaners. How much revenue is it generating? What are its expenses? How much profit is left over for the owners? Are there ways to increase the revenue, or decrease the expenses, or both? What does the competitive landscape look like? And after our evaluation, we'd then need to assess if the price of the 20% stake in the company was a good deal.

As with bonds, there are pros and cons to owning stock in the dry cleaners. The potential negatives are easy to see:

- We don't receive guaranteed interest payments.
- We don't have a contractual right to the return of our investment.
- Profits may not materialize as we expect.
- The business could go under if things got really bad.

That doesn't sound very appealing. Fortunately, there is a bright side to owning stock in a company. We get to share in the profits. Assuming the dry cleaners has a good year, it will have earned a profit. Management then decides how much of the profit to give back to the owners and how much to reinvest back into the company.

Profits returned to the company's owners are called **Dividends**. A dividend paid to owners is similar to interest paid to bondholders. There are, however, two big differences.

First, unlike interest payments on a bond, a company is usually not contractually obligated to pay dividends. Second, interest payments on a bond typically are fixed for the life of the bond. That's why rising interest rates hurt the value of existing bonds. With stock, however, dividends can go up as the profits of the company go up. Of course, they can also go down if profits fall.

So far, we've considered a fictional dry cleaners that you and I started. What we've learned, however, tells us everything we need to know about the world of investing in publicly traded companies. Just like our dry cleaners, we can invest in either stocks or bonds issued by companies like Apple, Microsoft, and General Motors. We can also invest in bonds issued by governments or municipalities. And the pros and cons of each are no different than with our dry cleaners. The companies and governments are just bigger.

So let's review.

Stock is ownership in a business. Buying one share of Apple, for example, would make you a part owner. You'd own a very, very, very small part of Apple. But you'd be an owner.

The terms Stock, Share, or Equity are interchangeable. They basically mean the same thing. When you hear a reporter refer to equities, as in "The equity market seems a bit overvalued," they are referring to stocks in general.

As a part owner of the business, you have a claim on the profits of the business. You can't literally control the profits. Remember, you own a very, very, very small percentage of the company. But you are still an owner.

When the management of a company like Apple decides to distribute some of the company's profits to its owners, it declares a dividend. That dividend gets paid out to you in proportion to your percentage of ownership. No different than our little dry cleaners.

A bond is a fancy word for debt. When the government issues a bond, it is borrowing money from investors who purchase the bond. Bonds are sometimes referred to as **Fixed Income**. Most bonds have a fixed interest rate paid out over a predictable schedule. Savings accounts and CDs are also fixed income investments.

Governments issue bonds, cleverly called **Government Bonds**. Corporations issue bonds, called **Corporate Bonds**. Local municipalities issue bonds, called—you guessed it—**Municipal Bonds**. You can impress your friends by referring to municipal bonds by their nickname, **Munis**.

Bonds entitle the bond holder to interest payments and the return of their initial investment when the bond reaches its maturity. Maturity is just a fancy word for the *term* of the Bond. You may have heard of a 5-year CD. Well, bonds have time limits too, ranging from just days to decades to even centuries (yep, some bonds mature 100 years after they are issued).

Stock and Bond Markets

So far, we've considered stocks and bonds of a single company or government. Now let's consider the entire market of stocks and bonds. If we look at how each of these **Asset Classes (a term that refers to different categories of investments)** has performed over the last 100 years or so, we learn two very important things:

First, stocks have performed better than bonds. Let's imagine that in 1928 we had $300 to invest. That's a lot of money today, but it was a small fortune in 1928. Anyway, let's split our money into three investments. We'll invest $100 in the stock of the 500 largest U.S. companies (tracked by what is known as the **S&P 500 Index**), $100 in three-month Treasury Bills issued by the U.S. government, and $100 in 10-year Treasury Bonds also issued by the U.S. government.

Any guess on how our investments performed? By the end of 2017, our investments would have grown to:

- 3-Month Treasury Bills: $2,105.63
- 10-Year Treasury Bonds: $7,309.87
- S&P 500 Stock Index: $399,885.98[28]

Historically, stocks outperform bonds.

---

28 http://pages.stern.nyu.edu/~adamodar/New_Home_Page/datafile/histretSP.html

Second, stock prices are more volatile than bond prices. In other words, the value of stocks swings up higher and down lower day-to-day, month-to-month, and year-to-year than the value of bonds.

Looking at the source noted above, for example, we can see that since 1928, three-month Treasury Bills have never gone down in value from one year to the next. They came close in 2011, earning just 0.03%. The T-bill's best year is one that I remember. In 1981 they earned 14.30%. Of course, unemployment was high and inflation was in the double-digits, giving birth to the term *stagflation*, but T-bills had a banner year.

The 10-year Treasury Bonds have had some losing years but not many. Seventeen years have seen negative returns since 1928. The worst year was 2009, when the 10-year bond lost 11.12%.

Stocks have had more bad years than bonds. The S&P 500 index has lost value in 25 years since 1928, and some of those years were ugly. The index lost 43.84% in 1931. More recently, in 2008, it lost 36.55%.

In the long run, stocks outperform bonds. But it's a bumpy ride.

And it's here, depending on your perspective, that you'll have one of two questions:

1. Since stocks do better than bonds in the long run, shouldn't I invest 100% of my money in stocks?
2. Since stocks can lose 30 or 40% in one year and bonds are more stable, shouldn't I invest 100% of my money in bonds?

Regardless of which question you ask, you likely have an additional question. How do I decide which stocks and bonds to invest in? Great questions. We need some more foundational information before we begin to answer these questions.

We'll start by looking at mutual funds.

3 KEY CONCEPTS

1. Stocks represent ownership in a company, while bonds are debt issued by government, municipalities and corporations.

2. In the long run, stocks perform better than bonds.

3. In the short term, stocks are more volatile than bonds.

CHAPTER 20

Mutual Funds

*"There seems to be some perverse human characteristic
that likes to make easy things difficult."*

– Warren Buffett

My father-in-law is amazing. As a young man, he served our country in the Navy. Afterward, he worked as an electrician for a company in Delaware and then started a commercial electrical contracting company.

He can build anything. He knows electrical work, of course, but his knowledge of everything from plumbing to HVAC, roofing to carpentry, is remarkable. And he built the house my wife grew up in.

It's hard for me to imagine building a house. I could hire a construction company to build a house, of course. But I can't imagine building one myself. Yet many people do.

Investing is similar. If you want to, you can pick individual stocks and bonds in which to invest your money. Many people do—just like some people build their own home. It's extremely time consuming and you need to know a lot about a lot of things.

As for the rest of us, we prefer to make investing easier. And that brings us to mutual funds. A **Mutual Fund** is an investment that holds hundreds, and sometimes thousands, of stocks, bonds, or both. An example of a mutual fund will help show you how they work.

Imagine you wanted to invest in the 500 largest public companies in the

U.S. Without mutual funds, you'd need to buy shares of each and every one of these companies. Just the fees alone on 500 transactions would cost you a fortune. And then there's the time involved in executing 500 orders. You'd also have to decide how much to invest in each company. Do you spread your money out evenly across all 500 companies, or do you invest more in the larger companies?

You'd also have to make changes in your investments over time. One of the 500 companies might get bought out by another one. Now you are down to 499 companies and you need to buy shares of whatever company now fills the 500th spot. Or perhaps one company goes bankrupt or falls out of the top 500 due to poor performance.

Mutual funds make this easy. There are funds that own shares of 500 of the largest U.S. companies and they follow the S&P 500 Index.[29] S&P is short for Standard & Poor's, the company behind the S&P 500 Index. By investing in shares of a mutual fund that tracks the S&P 500, you become an owner of each of the 500 companies. And you do this by owning shares of a single S&P 500 Index mutual fund (there are many of them to choose from, which we'll get to later). If the makeup of the 500 companies changes, the mutual fund changes the companies it owns to mirror that change. You don't have to do anything.

This is your first glimpse of the "press the button" simplicity of investing. But trust me, it gets much, much better.

Two Types of Mutual Funds

Broadly speaking, there are two types of mutual funds: **Actively Managed Mutual Funds** and **Index Mutual Funds**. It's important to understand the difference, which centers around how a mutual fund picks the stocks and bonds it holds.

---

29 https://www.spindices.com/indices/equity/sp-500

Actively Managed Funds

Let's start with actively managed funds. Some funds hire a team of finance professionals to evaluate investments. They try to pick the best stocks and bonds for the fund to own. They call these funds "actively managed" because these professionals are actively deciding how to invest your hard-earned money.

Here you may be wondering how else a fund might go about picking stocks and bonds. Are they going to hire a team of trained monkeys? If they did, some funds would actually improve their performance, but I'm getting ahead of myself.

Index Mutual Funds

No, some funds don't hire anybody to pick stocks and bonds. They simply track what is called an *index*. Perhaps the best known index is the S&P 500 Index, which we discussed just a moment ago. Index funds are also described as **Passive Investing** because a team of professionals isn't actively picking and choosing investments. They passively follow an index.

There are many indexes that track both stocks and bonds. Here are a few of the more popular ones:

- **Russell 3000**: Tracks 3,000 of the largest companies incorporated in the U.S..
- **Wilshire 5000**: Tracks all stocks currently trading in the U.S..
- **S&P Midcap 400**: Tracks U.S. companies with a market cap ranging from $1.4 to $4.9 billion.
- **FTSE All World Index**: Tracks over 3,000 companies in nearly 50 countries. FTSE stands for the Financial Times and London Stock Exchange, a joint venture that developed the index. You may hear FTSE pronounced "Foot-See," yet another way to impress your friends at the next party.

So which is better, you ask—actively managed mutual funds or index funds?

Oh, you've done it now. You've just stepped into one of the most contentious debates in all of investing.

As contentious as the debate may be, I can settle it with two words: *index funds*. If you gave me a few more words, I'd say the following: Over long periods of time, index funds outperform most actively managed funds on an after-fee and after-tax basis. But that's just the lawyer in me. My first answer was better: *index funds*.

A review of the performance of mutual funds over decades strongly favors index funds. In a recent Op-ed piece in *The Wall Street Journal*,[30] Burton Malkiel described the respective performance of actively managed funds compared to index funds:

- In 2016, two-thirds of actively managed mutual funds investing in large U.S. companies underperformed the S&P 500 Index.
- In the same year, 85% of actively managed mutual funds investing in small U.S. companies underperformed the S&P Small Cap Index.
- Over longer periods of 15 years, 90% of actively managed mutual funds underperform their respective indexes.
- Since 2001, 89% of actively managed international funds underperformed their respective indexes.

Now let's briefly cover why this is true. There are at least four reasons.

Fees: Index funds are cheaper than actively managed funds. Yes, mutual funds charge investors a fee. They don't send you a monthly invoice, however. They kindly take their fee out of your account. Actively managed funds are typically much more expensive than index funds.

In many cases, actively managed funds cost 1% a year, and sometimes more than 1%. Based on what you've already learned in this book, do you think a fee of even half that, say 0.50% a year, will matter much? How will that affect your journey to Level 7 Financial Freedom?

An actively managed fund that charges 1% in fees each year must beat the

---

30 https://www.wsj.com/articles/index-funds-still-beat-active-portfolio-management-1496701157

market by 1% just to break even. Most can't do this, and few if any can do it over decades.

We'll look at fees in more detail in the next chapter.

Taxes: Actively managed funds tend to buy and sell more stocks inside the fund. This activity can generate taxable gains for mutual fund shareholders. While this doesn't affect us in our retirement accounts, like a 401(k), it can put a big dent in our investments inside of our taxable accounts.

Cash: Actively managed funds tend to hold more cash than index funds. This too represents a drag on our performance. We don't need to pay an investment manager to hold our money in cash. We can do that ourselves in a savings account or certificate of deposit, thank you very much.

Performance: While actively managed funds hire professionals with impressive sounding credentials and degrees, most aren't capable of consistently beating the markets year after year. There are a few who can, like Warren Buffett, but most can't. Furthermore, it's impossible for us as investors to know ahead of time the one or two fund managers out of thousands who, 30 or 40 years from now, might beat the markets.

Index funds are like having your cake and eating it too. They are cheap, simple, and most outperform actively managed funds over the long run. Index mutual funds come in different shapes and sizes, and that's true for both stock index funds and bond index funds. Let's look at both.

Stock Index Funds

We categorize stock index funds in four ways (actively managed funds are also categorized in four way):

1. **Size**: Some index funds focus on small companies, some on big companies, and some on everything in between.

2. **Location**: Some funds focus on companies headquartered in the U.S., some on companies outside the U.S., and some in specific regions of the world.

3. **Valuation**: Some funds focus on companies that appear to be under-valued, while some funds focus on companies that are in a growth spurt.

4. **Specialty**: Some funds focus on specific types of investments, such as real estate or commodities.

Size

Public companies come in all sizes. These are extremely large companies, such as Apple. As of this writing, its Market Valuation (the number of shares owned by the public multiplied by the price of a single share) exceeds $800 billion. The fancy-pants term for a company's value is **Market Capitalization**, or **Market Cap** for short.

There are also very small public companies. You and I haven't heard of most of these businesses, but we have heard of some of them. As an example, you may have heard of Brinks, the armored car company. It's considered a **Small-Cap** company. Why? Its market cap is about $3.5 billion. That's a lot of money to you and me but not compared to companies worth hundreds of billions of dollars.

Large companies like Apple are referred to as **Large-Cap** companies, referring to their market capitalization. It's large. Thus, large cap. Really complicated, I know.

There are also **Mid-Cap** companies, those like the Goldilocks story where things are not too big and not too small.

Not to be out done, really, really small companies are sometimes referred to as **Micro-Cap** companies. Yeah, Wall Street is full of itself. But you get the idea.

I know what you are thinking. "Rob, I really appreciate all your effort here. Thanks for the lesson on market cap. But so what? Who cares?"

We care for two very different reasons.

First, as you enter the world of investing, you will hear about and read about market cap. You need to know what that means in order to understand what you are hearing and reading. At a minimum, you won't be intimidated by the jargon and you'll understand why you are "pressing the button." For example, your 401(k) may offer a mutual fund that invests in small-, mid-, or large-cap companies. Now you know what those terms mean.

Second, history tells us that the returns of large-cap and small-cap companies are different. So is the volatility—i.e., the price swings in the market price of these companies. Generally, small-cap stocks have a higher return than large-cap stocks over a long period of time. That's the good news. They also have greater volatility. Think of small-cap stocks as a wild roller coaster ride. That's the bad news.

Location

Stocks can also be divided based on where a company is headquartered. Companies headquartered in the good ol' U.S. of A are cleverly referred to as U.S. companies.

Companies headquartered outside of the U.S. go by several names. They are referred to generally as **International** or **Foreign** companies (at least by those of us in the U.S.).

International stocks are further divided into companies headquartered in **Developed Countries** and those in **Emerging Markets**. Developed countries have mature economies, like Germany. Emerging markets have less mature economies, like India.

Now, notice that I've focused on where companies are headquartered, not where they do business. Companies in the twenty-first century do business everywhere. While Apple is a U.S. company headquartered in Cupertino, California, it does business all over the globe.

As globalization continues, the distinction between U.S. companies and International companies diminishes. Still, it's a distinction we'll need to keep in mind as you'll see. Some mutual funds focus exclusively on U.S. companies and some on international companies. Some focus on emerging markets and some invest across the globe.

Valuation

Mutual funds can also focus on either **Growth** or **Value** stocks. Growth stocks are those of companies whose revenue is growing rapidly. Here a company like Amazon comes to mind. In contrast, value stocks are those of companies whose stock price is considered undervalued. Here a company like Ford comes to mind.

Growth stocks are the high flyers. They are the companies in the news and discussed at water coolers everywhere. In addition to Amazon, Tesla and Netflix are examples of growth stocks. They are also very expensive compared to the profits, if any, that they generate.

Value stocks are often the older companies. Some would even describe them as boring. In addition to Ford, value companies include the likes of General Electric and Procter & Gamble.

Some mutual funds invest in both growth and value stocks. An example of this type of fund is an S&P 500 Index fund. The 500 large companies includes both growth and value companies. This type of fund is sometimes referred to as a **Blend** of growth and value, since it invests in both.

Now imagine you encounter a U.S. Small Cap Value mutual fund. Any idea what types of companies make up its portfolio of investments? Now you know. It invests in small companies headquartered in the U.S. that are considered undervalued. And yes, these types of funds exist.

To give you a real-world example, consider the Vanguard Small-Cap Value Index Fund. Its **Ticker**, a unique set of letters that identifies the fund, is VISVX (you'll see why tickers are important in the next chapter). Here's how Vanguard describes this mutual fund:

"This low-cost index fund offers exposure to small-capitalization U.S. value stocks. Value stocks are those that may be temporarily undervalued by investors. These companies typically grow at a slower pace than the typical company. The fund seeks to track a value-style index of small-sized companies. One of the fund's primary risks is its focus on the small-cap arena, which is an often-volatile segment of the market. Investors looking to add a passively managed, small-cap value allocation to an already diversified portfolio may wish to consider this fund."

Given what we've already covered, you should follow this description like a pro.

Specialty

Some mutual funds invest in specific assets or industries. Two important examples of specialty funds are REITs and Commodity funds.

A **REIT**, or Real Estate Investment Trust, is a mutual fund that invests in real estate. REIT funds can focus on apartment buildings, retail space, shopping malls, commercial property, and even mortgages.

Tax Alert: An important detail to remember is that REIT funds are not tax efficient. They pay out a substantial portion of their profits each year, and these distributions are taxed as ordinary income. As a result, if you invest in a REIT fund, you should do so inside a *retirement* account.

Commodity funds invest in **commodities**. Here think of oil, corn, gold, and so on. Some funds invest directly in the commodity, while others invest in companies whose performance depends in large measure on the price of commodities (e.g., an oil or mining company).

Bond Mutual Funds

Just like stocks, bond mutual funds come in several flavors.

1. **Borrower**: Governments, corporations, and local municipalities all issue bonds.
2. **Location**: Just like stocks, bonds can be issued by borrowers in the U.S or anywhere in the world.
3. **Credit Risk**: The risk that a borrower will fail to repay the interest, principal, or both, on time. Particularly in the world of corporate bonds, some funds focus on bonds issued by financially strong companies, while others focus on bonds issued by companies with shaky financials.
4. **Interest Rate Risk**: The risk that interest rates will rise, depressing the value of existing, lower rate bonds. To address this risk, some mutual

funds invest in shorter-term bonds, while others invest in bonds that protect investors against rising rates.

Borrower

Mutual funds focus on bonds issued by different borrowers. Some funds focus on government bonds, some on corporate bonds, and some on "munis." And then there are bond funds that invest in all three.

Location

Some funds focus on bonds issued by U.S. governments, corporations and/ or municipalities. Some funds focus on bonds issued by entities outside of the U.S. And not to be outdone, some funds invest in both.

Credit Risk

As we know, credit risk refers to the risk that a borrower will default. U.S. government bonds are considered the safest with no chance that it will fail to repay its debts (let's hope prevailing wisdom is right). In contrast, a bond issued by a third world country would have a higher risk of default.

Corporate bonds are similar. A bond issued by Apple would have a very low risk of default. Apple has an excellent balance sheet, strong revenues and profit, and a mountain of cash in the bank. In contrast, a bond issued by Sprint has a greater risk of default.

You might wonder why anybody would invest in a bond issued by a government or corporation that has a higher risk of default. In a word—yield. **Yield** is a fancy word for interest rate. The higher the credit risk, the higher the yield.

In fact, mutual funds that invest in corporate bonds issued by companies with shaky financials are called **High Yield** bond funds. High yield bonds are also called **Junk Bonds**. To be clear, junk bonds are not junk. They have more risk, but they also have potentially more reward.

Interest Rate Risk

Most bonds don't protect you against the risk that interest rates will rise. Recall that as rates rise, the value of existing lower-yielding bonds fall. There are some bonds, however, that do protect investors against rising rates. They do so in one of two ways:

First, some bonds offer protection against rising rates. How? They pay investors a higher yield as inflation and interest rates rise. What are these magical bonds?

Issued by the U.S. government, both **TIPS** (Treasury Inflation-Protected Securities) and **I Bonds** have unique features. As inflation and interest rates rise, so do the rates on both TIPS and I Bonds. Given this, you may wonder why anybody would invest in other types of bonds.

Remember this: There is no free lunch. Yes, TIPS and I Bonds protect an investor against rising rates, but they do so at a cost. Think of this interest rate risk protection as insurance that you must buy. You "buy" it by accepting a lower starting yield on both TIPS and I Bonds. This insurance is worth the lower yield if rates do in fact rise more than anticipated. If they don't, however, you've accepted a lower yield for nothing in return.

Second, some bond funds protect against interest rate risk by investing in short-term bonds. This strategy doesn't result in higher yields when inflation rises. Instead, it limits your interest rate risk because the bonds mature in the near future (think months or a year or two). If interest rates rise, would you rather be "stuck" in a six-month bond at a lower rate or a 30-year bond at a lower rate?

The key term here is **Duration**. Bond mutual funds have a stated duration, which, generally speaking, refers to the weighted average time it will take all the bonds in the mutual fund to pay back the interest and the principal to investors. The details aren't important. What is important is that the longer a bond fund's duration, the higher the interest rate risk.

Here we can think of bond funds as being short term, intermediate term, or long term. While there isn't one official definition of these terms, here's a general guideline: A **Short Term** bond fund is one with a duration of less than three years. A short term bond fund's interest rate risk would be considered low. An **Intermediate Term** bond fund is one with an average duration of about three to 10 years. And a **Long Term** bond fund has an average duration of more than 10 years.

3 KEY TAKEAWAYS

1. Mutual funds make investing easier by enabling us to invest in thousands of stocks or bonds through a single investment in a fund.

2. There are two types of mutual funds: Actively managed funds and index funds. Index funds outperform most actively managed funds over the long term.

3. Stock and bond mutual funds come in different shapes and sizes.

CHAPTER 21

Mutual Fund Fees

"Most institutional and individual investors will find the best way to own common stock is through an index fund that charges minimal fees."

— Warren Buffet

Recall that we started our journey together talking about the Matrix. The Matrix tricked people into thinking everything was right in the world when it wasn't. Investing fees are just like the Matrix.

On the surface they look harmless. How bad can a 1% fee really be? We can earn more than that from a cash back credit card. Yet as harmless as "small" investment fees may seem, they will eat the heart and soul out of any well-meaning Freedom Fighter. Yes, it's that serious.

It's easy to find excellent low-fee investments. In fact, history tells us **the lower the cost of investment, the better it will perform in the long run.**[31] It's counterintuitive because we are conditioned to believe that we get what we pay for. But this is not true when it comes to investing.

In this chapter we'll look at three types of mutual fund fees. Then we'll look at why fees matter so much. Finally, I'll give you some guidance on what is a reasonable fee.

---

31 https://personal.vanguard.com/pdf/morningstar.pdf

Expense Ratio

As we've discussed in the previous chapters, mutual funds are not free. You have to pay fees to the management company for the work they do to construct and run the mutual fund. Mutual fund fees come in different flavors, but virtually all funds charge what is called an Expense Ratio.

An Expense Ratio represents the percentage of your investments that the mutual fund company will take as a fee. For example, an Expense Ratio of 1% will cost you one percent of your portfolio every year ($100 for every $10,000 invested). Expense Ratios are often expressed in **Basis Points** or **Bips** for short. One hundred basis points equals 1%. Fifty basis points equal 0.50%. Expense Ratios range from just a few Bips (e.g., 0.05%) to well over 200 (2%).

Transaction Costs

Mutual funds pay fees to buy and sell stocks and bonds. In this way, they are no different than if you and I bought and sold individual stocks and bonds. We'd have to pay a brokerage fee. So do mutual funds.

Here's the dirty little secret few people know. The transaction costs that mutual funds pay do not come out of the Expense Ratio we just looked at. They are a separate fee. What's more, we don't know ahead of time what those fees will be. Why? Because not even the mutual funds know what their transaction costs will be until they actually decide to buy or sell something.

We can, if we want, see what a mutual fund company paid in the past for transaction costs. We'd do that by digging into what is called a **Statement of Additional Information**. These are dense impenetrable documents filed with the Securities and Exchange Commission in Washington, DC.

Here's what you need to know. Index funds tend to have far fewer transaction costs than actively managed funds. Once again, index funds win out over actively managed funds.

Load Fees

Some, but not all, mutual funds charge what are called Load Fees. These are fees you pay when you either buy shares of the fund or sell shares of the fund. Front-End Load Fees apply when you buy shares of a mutual fund. Back End Load Fees apply when you sell shares of a mutual fund.

A typical Front-End Load Fee is 5.75% of the amount you invest. Funds with Load Fees also charge higher Expense Ratios than most index funds. These Load Fees and higher Expense Ratios go, in part, to pay the investment advisors who sell these funds to investors.

The index funds that I recommend don't charge Load Fees.

Why Fees Matter

I can remember one of the first investments I ever made. What a mistake.

I bought the investment from a bank. I didn't know what I was doing and I invested in an actively managed fund with a 5.75% Front-End Load Fee. Yikes! On top of that, the fund charged an annual Expense Ratio of more than 1%. Double Yikes!

Let's put those numbers into perspective. Recall from the chapter on the Money Multiplier that if we invest $208 a month at 9.3%, we'll end up with $1,708,072.76 after 45 years. What happens when we apply a 5.75% Load Fee and a 1% expense ratio?

For starters, we lose $11.96 from our monthly $208 investment thanks to the Load Fee. Thus, we are investing $196.04 a month after the Load Fee. Second, our after-fee returns drop by the 1% expense ratio. So we net 8.3%. And the result…$1,143.727.39.

Those "small" fees cost us 33% of our wealth, or $564,345.37. That's why I say that friends don't let friends pay high investment fees.

Now let's look at this from the perspective of Level 7 Financial Freedom. Recall that it will take us about 31 years to reach Level 7 based on the following assumptions:

- Annual Income: $75,000
- Saving Rate: 20% ($15,000 a year)
- Spending Rate: 80% ($60,000 a year)
- Real Return: 6.3%

Applying the above "small" fees, our numbers change as follows:

- Annual Income: $75,000
- Saving Rate: 18.85% ($15,000 a year - 5.75% Load Fee = $14,137.50)
- Spending Rate: 80% ($60,000 a year)
- Real Return: 5.3% (after 1% Expense Ratio)

If it takes 31 years *without* these fees, how much does it take *with* these fees? About 36 years. A few small fees translate into over four years of hard labor. Yeah, fees matter.

This brings us to two really important questions:

1. When it comes to fees, what's reasonable?
2. How do we keep our fees as low as possible?

1. What's a reasonable fee for a mutual fund?

As you now know, mutual funds come in two flavors: Actively managed funds and index funds. With few exceptions, actively managed funds are more expensive than index funds.

For actively managed funds, we want the Expense Ratio to be below 75 basis points (that's 0.75%). As you know, I recommend index funds. For me, even 75 basis points is just too expensive. But if you plan to invest in actively managed funds, don't pay more than 75 basis points. And expense ratios closer to 50 basis points are even better.

For index funds, we want the Expense Ratio to be below 25 basis points (that's 0.25%), and preferably below 10 basis points. The best index funds from the likes of Vanguard and Fidelity cost less than five basis points. And Fidelity has recently started offering index funds for free.

And of course, we never want to invest in a mutual fund that charges Load Fees.

2. How do we keep our fees as low as possible?

The simple answer is: Stick to index funds. Not only are they less expensive but as we've discussed, they outperform the vast majority of actively managed funds over the long term.

Fees are critical. We need to keep them as low as possible so that our money can work for *us*, not for a mutual fund company or investment advisor.

3 KEY CONCEPTS

1. Fees are one of the few things investors can control.

2. High fees can add years, even a decade, to the time it takes you to reach Level 7 Financial Freedom.

3. Index funds offer both low fees and better performance.

CHAPTER 22

Investing Made Easy

"Make everything as simple as possible, but not simpler."
– Albert Einstein

I f the last few chapters have your head spinning, this chapter will bring you back down to earth. We are going to look at some very simple yet effective ways to invest. As you'll see, you can literally build an incredible investment portfolio with just one mutual fund.

Let's begin with what we want our investment portfolio to look like.

Our Goal

We have just four goals to keep in mind as we decide how to invest.

1. **Diversification**: We don't want to put all of our eggs in one basket. We have no idea whether U.S. stocks or foreign stocks will do better over the next few decades. The same is true for big or small companies. How will REITs perform? I have no idea. Because we don't know the future, we want to cover all of our bases. We do that by investing in different asset classes. As you'll see, that's very easy to do.

2. **Equities**: History tells us that stocks outperform bonds over the long term. We already know how this difference would affect our journey to Level 7 Financial Freedom. The point is this: we want more of our money invested in stocks than we have invested in bonds.

3. **Low Cost**: We want to keep our costs as low as possible. It's one of the reasons we favor index funds over actively managed funds.

4. **Simplicity**: Finally, we want to keep it simple. There are really complicated ways to invest, just like there are complicated ways to do just about anything. We value simplicity. It's easier to understand and manage. And besides, life is complicated enough.

So how do we put all of this together? It's easy, and there are several ways to do it. We'll start with one of my favorites—target date retirement funds.

Target Date Retirement Funds

Mutual fund companies had a bright idea several years ago. They decided to create mutual funds that made investing incredibly simple. By investing in just *one* mutual fund, you can get great diversification, a portfolio with plenty of exposure to stocks, and low costs.

To show you how they work, I'm going to use Vanguard's Target-Date Retirement Funds (TDR) as an example. Let's assume you are 25 and plan to work for 40 years until you are 65. In 2019, that means you'll retire in 2059. Vanguard offers target date retirement funds by year. In our example, we might pick the 2060 fund (they go up in five-year increments). The fund's official name is the Vanguard Target Retirement 2060 Fund (VTTSX).

You contribute to this single fund. It's your only investment. At first it may not seem like we are well diversified. How diversified can you be in a single mutual fund? **Very**.

Vanguard takes your money and divides it into four different Vanguard mutual funds for you. Here they are:

1. Vanguard Total Stock Market Index Fund Investor Shares (54.6%)
2. Vanguard Total International Stock Index Fund Investor Shares (35.4%)
3. Vanguard Total Bond Market II Index Fund Investor Shares (7.00%)
4. Vanguard Total International Bond Index Fund Investor Shares (3.00%)

Even with four funds, you may be questioning just how diversified this portfolio really is. One thing to always keep in mind is that the number of mutual funds, by itself, tells you nothing about how well diversified a portfolio is. You must look at what the fund(s) invests in. And it's easy to do.

Using the free tools from Morningstar, we can see how the Vanguard Target Retirement 2060 Fund invests money. The ticker for this fund is VTTSX. As we saw earlier, a **Ticker** is a unique set of letters that identities every mutual fund (they also identify every stock or other security. Apple, for example, trades under the ticker AAPL). Searching the ticker VTTSX in Morningstar.com brings up a wealth of information.

The results confirm that the 2060 fund does invest in the four mutual funds listed above, and we can then dive into each of these funds. The Vanguard Total International Stock Index Fund (VGTSX), for example, invests in over 6,000 different companies. The Vanguard Total Bond Market II Index Fund (VTBIX) invests in over 13,000 bonds. We can also see that these investments cover big and small companies, U.S. and foreign companies, and value and growth companies. Yes, we're diversified.

> **Note**: Morningstar is an excellent and free source of information on mutual funds. We'll walk through an example of how to use it in the chapter on How to Evaluate a Mutual Fund.

The Vanguard 2060 Fund is also inexpensive. Its Expense Ratio is just 0.15% (or 15 basis points), and it charges no Load Fees. And the minimum investment is just $1,000.

There are two other significant benefits to target date retirement funds. First, they rebalance for you automatically. Second, they shift your portfolio toward bonds as you near retirement. The idea is to make your portfolio less susceptible to wild stock market swings as you get closer to needing the money.

Let's look at both of these features.

Rebalancing

Let's imagine you wanted to invest 70% of your money in stocks and 30% in bonds. You pick out your mutual funds, invest your money, and all is right in the world.

Then the market opens and the value of stocks and bonds goes up and down. Why? Because that's what they do. In short order, you no longer have a 70/30 portfolio. At first it may not shift much. Perhaps in a month you have a 69.5/30.5 portfolio. Not a big deal.

But give it some time, and depending on how the stock and bond markets perform, your portfolio can shift significantly from your 70/30 plan. Rebalancing simply means buying and selling investments to bring your portfolio back to your planned allocation.

With a Target Date Retirement Fund, you don't have to worry about rebalancing. The fund does it for you.

Retirement Investing

Target Date Retirement Funds shift your portfolio more toward bonds and away from stocks as you near retirement. To be clear, you will still be invested in stocks. Even in retirement, your portfolio will be heavily invested in equities. You need the returns they provide so you don't run out of money, even following the 4% Rule. But the portfolio moves more into bonds as you near and enter retirement.

Here's an example. The 2060 fund today invests about 90% of every dollar in stock funds and 10% in bond funds. Let's compare that to the 2020 fund, which is designed for people about to retire. The 2020 fund invests 53% in stocks and 47% in bonds. Still a lot invested in stocks, but a big shift toward bonds compared to the 2060 fund.

The point is that TDR funds do this for you as you age. They truly are "set it and forget it" mutual funds. They are by far the easiest way to invest. They are not, however, the *only* way to invest. There are other approaches that are easy as well.

But why would we consider alternatives? Good question. And there are several reasons.

First, you may want more control over your investments. TDR funds are simple because they make most of the decisions for you. However, you may want to make some of these decisions on your own.

Second, your 401(k) or other workplace retirement account may not offer TDR funds. That's unlikely today, but possible. Or they may offer TDR funds that you don't like. Some TDRs charge outrageous fees.

Third, Target Date Retirement funds have a drawback in taxable accounts. As you saw above, they include bond mutual funds, which generally should be kept in retirement accounts for tax reasons (bond funds pay interest which is taxable if held outside a retirement fund).

Finally, TDR funds do come at a cost. While the good ones, like those offered by Vanguard, are relatively inexpensive, they are more expensive than investing directly in other index funds. And the bad TDR funds can get really expensive.

So, let's look at some alternatives…

TDR + 1

If you want to add a bit of flexibility to your investments but keep the simplicity of a TDR, the TDR + 1 strategy may do the trick. It's simple. You invest in a TDR plus one additional fund that covers an investing style that's important to you.

As an example, investor Paul Merriman recommends a portfolio consisting of a TDR + a small cap value mutual fund.[32] A good example of such a fund is the Vanguard Small-Cap Value Index Fund (VISVX). I've owned this fund in the past. With this approach, you might invest 90% of your money in the

---

32 https://paulmerriman.com/2-funds-for-life/

Vanguard 2060 fund and 10% in the Vanguard small cap fund.

3-Fund Portfolio

Our next option involves just three mutual funds. It's an approach popularized by a group of investors called the Bogleheads. Don't let the name fool you. This is a serious group of passionate and knowledgeable investors. They named their group after Vanguard's founder, John Bogle. They even have a conference each year.

The 3-Fund Portfolio requires three types of index mutual funds:

- U.S. Stocks
- Foreign Stocks
- U.S. Bonds

That's it. Now the big question. How much money do you put in each type of fund?

One option would be to follow what Vanguard does in its TDR funds. You'd find the fund that corresponds to when you plan to retire and mimic the same allocation. For example, the Vanguard 2040 TDR fund invests 51% in U.S. Stocks, 34% in Foreign Stocks, and the rest in bonds. You can find information on Vanguard's TDR funds here: https://www.retirebeforemomanddad.com/Vanguard_TDR.

In my opinion, an 80/20 portfolio is ideal for long-term investors (those who don't need the money for at least 10 years). As such, I believe the following portfolio of Vanguard funds is an excellent 3-Fund Portfolio:

- 50%: Vanguard Total Stock Market Index Fund (VTSAX)
- 30%: Vanguard Total International Stock Index Fund (VTIAX)
- 20%: Vanguard Total Bond Index Fund (VBTLX)

You'll find examples of the 3-Fund Portfolio using index funds from the major mutual fund companies on the Bogleheads' website: https://www.retire-beforemomanddad.com/3-fund-portfolio.

I want to stress one thing. Don't overthink your stock to bond allocation. It's as much art as science. I believe that for the long-term investors, 80/20 is ideal. That said, 70/30 is reasonable, as is 90/10.

6-Fund Portfolio

I'll mention one more option for those with an adventurous spirit. This is the portfolio I've used for years. Here are the investment types with the percentages of assets that I invested in each:

- U.S. Large Cap Stocks (30%)
- U.S. Small Cap Value Stocks (10%)
- U.S. Bonds (20%)
- Foreign Developed Country Stocks (20%)
- Emerging Market Stocks (10%)
- REITs (10%)

Here are the specific funds I used to create my 6-Fund Portfolio:

- Vanguard 500 Index Fund Admiral Shares (FVIAX)
- Vanguard Emerging Markets Stock Index Fund Admiral Shares (VEMAX)
- Vanguard Developed Markets Index Fund Admiral Shares (VTMGX)
- Vanguard Intermediate-Term Bond Index Fund Admiral Shares (VBILX)
- Vanguard Real Estate Index Fund Admiral Shares (VGSLX)
- Vanguard Small Cap Value Index Fund Admiral Shares (VSIAX)

This approach does take more work. Remember, as market values change, you need to rebalance your portfolio from time to time. Once a year is more than enough. It's not a lot of work, but it's work. A TDR Fund is easier.

So which one should you pick? There is no "right" answer. For those starting out, I think a TDR Fund inside a retirement account is a great solution. Ultimately, you want to go with a portfolio that you'll stick to no matter how the market performs (more on that in the chapter about "You").

Finally, a word about Vanguard. You may have noticed that most of my examples in this book use Vanguard index funds. I use them as examples because that's where I've kept most of our portfolio for the past three decades. Vanguard invented the index fund as we know it today, and I believe they truly put investors first.

That being said, there are other great options available to investors. As my good friend Rick Ferri (https://core-4.com) has pointed out, index funds and ETFs offered by Schwab, Fidelity, and TD Ameritrade have leveled the playing field. The key is understanding how to evaluate a mutual fund, which we will cover shortly. But first, let's turn to retirement accounts.

3 KEY TAKEAWAYS

1. There are several simple and effective ways to invest, including Target Date Retirement Funds and the 3-Fund Portfolio.

2. There is no one "right" way to invest. Much of the decision comes down to your personality and the funds available in your employer's retirement account.

3. Whatever approach you choose, stick to it.

Video: https://www.retirebeforemomanddad.com/Chapter22

CHAPTER 23

Retirement Accounts

"Don't simply retire from something; have something to retire to."
— Harry Emerson Fosdick

You're excited about the journey to Financial Freedom. You've mastered the Money Multiplier. You've slashed your expenses without major sacrifice by using The Money Audit. You've chosen your investment strategy from the last chapter. You're ready to invest.

Now what do you do? Do you invest in your company's 401(k)? Do you open an IRA? Are you wondering about Roth retirement accounts that you may have heard about? And you could always open a simple taxable account.

What. Do. You. Do?

In this chapter I'll give you a simple plan of attack that will enable you to navigate these waters, and it's easy to execute.

First, we'll get an overview of the primary types of retirement accounts most people will encounter. We need to understand how they work so we can put them to work for us.

Second, I'll lay out the plan. Then we'll dive into understanding why the plan works and also how you might individualize it for your specific circumstances.

Finally, we'll cover some exceptions. There are circumstances where you might want to deviate from the plan. We'll talk about those and why they might apply to you.

Retirement Accounts

Retirement accounts fall into three primary categories:

1. **Workplace Retirement Accounts**: These are accounts offered by your employer.
2. **Individual Retirement Accounts**: These are accounts you can open on your own.
3. **Health Savings Accounts**: These are accounts you can open if you have a High Deductible Health Plan (and yes, they can be a powerful part of your Level 7 journey).

Let's look at each type of account.

Workplace Retirement Accounts

As the name suggests, these are retirement accounts offered by your employer. The two most common are 401(k) and 403(b) accounts. Ever wonder why these accounts have such arcane names? Probably not, because, let's be honest, who really cares? But for the few of you who do (and that includes me), these names refer to the sections of the tax code that authorize these types of retirement accounts.

Most government employees, military personnel, and postal workers have the Thrift Savings Plan, or TSP. It's the government's version of a 401(k). State and local government employees may have access to a 457 plan, which is very similar to a 401(k).

Going forward, I'll simply refer to 401(k)s or workplace retirement accounts. The principles we'll cover, however, apply to all of the various accounts mentioned above.

There is an annual limit to how much you can contribute to a 401(k). In 2019 that limit is $19,000. The limit is indexed to inflation, so it can go up from year to year. In addition, those 50 or older by the end of the year can also make what is called a catch-up contribution. In 2019 the catch-up contribution limit is $6,000.

Your employer decides which company will manage its retirement account on behalf of its employees. It also decides which investments will be available to employees who contribute to their 401(k). Finally, some employers contribute to their employees' retirement accounts, typically matching a percentage of an employee's contributions.

Traditional vs. Roth 401(k) Accounts

The 401(k) accounts come in two flavors—a 401(k), sometimes called a Traditional 401(k), and a Roth 401(k). While the contribution limits are the same, the tax benefits are vastly different.

With a Traditional 401(k), the amount of your contribution is deducted from your taxable income for both state and federal income taxes. For example, let's assume you contribute $10,000 to a 401(k) this year. Let's also assume your combined state and federal marginal tax rate[33] is 25%. Your $10,000 contribution will reduce your tax bill by $2,500.

There is no free lunch, however. When you take the money out of the account, the amount of the distribution is taxed as ordinary income. That's true when you take out the contributions you made to the account. It's also true when you take out any earnings on those contributions that your investments generated. In effect, a 401(k) enables you to defer paying the income tax until you take a distribution from the account, which can be decades later.

Contributions to a Roth 401(k) are **not** deducted from your taxable income. You pay taxes on the amount as if you had never made the contribution. Qualified distributions from the account, however, are tax free. At this point you may be saying, "So what? Since I didn't get a tax break when I contributed to the Roth 401(k), I would sure hope the government wouldn't tax me when I

---

33 Your marginal tax rate is the percentage you pay in taxes on your last dollar of taxable income. Remember that federal income tax brackets are progressive; the more you make, the higher your tax rate. Your marginal rate is the highest rate you pay based on your income. We use marginal rates here because had you not made a 401(k) contribution, that money would have been added to your taxable income and taxed at whatever rate corresponded with your income.

take the money out."

True. But here's the benefit. Not only are your contributions tax free when you later take them out in retirement, but so are your investment earnings generated from your contributions.

Imagine making a $10,000 investment at age 25. Forty years later, assuming a 9.3% return, that 10 grand is now worth $406,768.46. And it's all tax free.

So after all this, you may be asking which is better – a Traditional 401(k) or a Roth 401(k)? In short, for most people, the answer is a Roth 401(k). I'll explain why in just a bit, along with some exceptions. First, let's turn to IRAs.

Individual Retirement Accounts

An Individual Retirement Account, or IRA, is a tax advantaged retirement account you set up yourself. Because *you* open the account, as opposed to your employer, *you* get to decide where to open the account and what investments to include in your account.

The contribution limits for an IRA are lower than they are for a 401(k). In 2019, the IRA contribution limit is $6,000. As with a 401(k), those 50 or older can make a catch-up contribution to an IRA. The 2019 limit for the catch-up contribution is $1,000.

As with a 401(k), an IRA comes in two flavors—a Traditional IRA and a Roth IRA. As you'll see, the rules surrounding IRAs are a bit more complicated than those for a 401(k).

Traditional IRA

With an IRA, your contributions are deductible from your taxable income if you meet certain requirements. Recall that contributions to a 401(k) are deductible, period. In fact, 401(k) contributions don't even show up as taxable income on your W-2. Your employer deducts them for you.

Not so with an IRA. Because there is no employer involved, your W-2 won't reflect any contributions you make to an IRA. Instead, you have to deduct them yourself on your tax return. But you can only do this if you qualify for the deduction.

In 2019, if your filing status is single or head of household, you can deduct your IRA contributions from your taxable income if, and only if:

- You are not covered by a workplace retirement plan, OR
- You are covered by a workplace retirement plan, but your modified adjusted gross income (MAGI) is less than $64,000.

As your MAGI rises above $64,000, the amount of your contribution that you can deduct decreases. Once your MAGI hits $74,000, none of your IRA contribution is deductible. Keep in mind that these numbers change every year.

In 2019, if you are married and filing joint tax returns, you can deduct your IRA contributions from your taxable income if, and only if:

- Neither you nor your spouse are covered by a workplace retirement plan, OR
- You are covered by a workplace retirement plan, but your MAGI is less than $103,000 (above this, your deduction is phased out and no deduction is permitted once your MAGI reaches $123,000), OR
- You are not covered by a workplace retirement plan, but your spouse is, and your MAGI is less than $193,000 (above this, your deduction is phased out and no deduction is permitted once your MAGI reaches $203,000).

Is your head spinning? Yeah, you can thank our fearless leaders in Washington for this mess. You should also consult your neighborhood tax preparer or favorite tax software to confirm whether your IRA contributions are deductible. Note that the above MAGI numbers change from year to year based on inflation.

If you cannot deduct contributions to an IRA, and in some cases even if you can, a Roth IRA may be a better option.

Roth IRA

Roth IRA contributions, like Roth 401(k) contributions, are not deductible. That means we don't need to wade through all the crazy rules for deductibility like we do with a Traditional IRA. And like a Roth 401(k), you don't pay taxes on qualified distributions in retirement, and you can always take out your contributions tax and penalty free. But if you withdraw earnings before you turn 59.5 years old, you'll pay the 10% penalty tax AND income tax (with some exceptions).

There is one catch. It's possible for you to make too much money to qualify for a Roth IRA. In 2019, for singles and heads of household, the phase-out range is $122,000 to $137,000. If you are married and filing jointly, the phase-out range is $193,000 to $203,000. If these incomes disqualify you, there is another way to fund a Roth IRA, and it's sometimes called a **Backdoor Roth IRA**.

Here's how it works. First you contribute to a Traditional IRA. Then you transfer the money from your Traditional IRA to a Roth IRA. This is called a Roth IRA conversion. Because you didn't take a tax deduction on your initial contribution to your Traditional IRA, the conversion does not trigger any tax liability. (If your contribution grew in value from the time of your contribution to the time of the Roth IRA conversion, the increase in value would be taxed as ordinary income. If the conversion happens soon after the IRA contribution, however, this amount should be minimal.)

Here we need to distinguish between Roth IRA **Contributions** and Roth IRA **Conversions**. Each method enables us to add money to a Roth IRA. But the methods are different and they come with a different set of rules. What you need to know is that Roth IRA *Contributions* can always be withdrawn at any time without tax or penalty. But with Roth IRA *Conversions*, you must wait five years.

To learn more about a Backdoor Roth IRA and the 5-year rule, I recommend this article from Michael Kitces, CFP: "Understanding the Two 5-Year Rules for Roth IRA Contributions and Conversions." Always keep in mind, however, that tax laws are tricky and can change. So consult a tax advisor.

Before we leave Backdoor Roth IRAs, we need to drag one more complication out of the dark closet. You may have several Traditional IRA accounts. The IRS treats them as one for many purposes. For example, you may have an IRA for which you've taken tax deductions on your contributions over the years. Now as your income has gone up, you no longer qualify for the deduction on new contributions and cannot contribute directly to a Roth IRA, either.

So you decide to open a new IRA, contribute to it, and then execute the Backdoor Roth IRA strategy. Wait a minute—not so fast. While you never touched the old deductible IRA, the IRS will nevertheless combine it with your new IRA to determine how much of the conversion came from your old deductible IRA contributions and how much came from your new nondeductible contributions.

Let's assume you have $5,000 in a deductible IRA and you contribute $5,000 to a new nondeductible IRA. When you convert this new IRA to a Roth IRA, the IRS will treat it as $2,500 having come from your deductible IRA, and $2,500 from your new nondeductible IRA. The $2,500 from your old deductible IRA will be treated as taxable income.[34]

Health Savings Account (HSA)

An HSA is a tax advantaged account designed to help you pay for medical expenses. You can fund an HSA if, and only if, you have a high deductible health plan (HDHP). The IRS releases each year the amount of the deductible necessary for a health insurance plan to qualify as an HDHP. The good news is you don't need to know the numbers. A health insurance plan through your employer or one you buy on your own will tell you whether it is an HDHP that qualifies for an HSA (you probably hate TLAs by now—Three Letter Acronyms).

---

34 For more on the Backdoor Roth IRA and potential gotchas, check out this from Ashlea Ebeling at Forbes: https://www.forbes.com/sites/ashleaebeling/2018/01/22/congress-blesses-roth-iras-for-everyone-even-the-well-paid/#5119c0467471

For those of you who love numbers, however, in 2019 an HDHP is one in which the deductible is at least:

- $1,350 for individuals
- $2,700 for families

If you have a qualifying HDHP, you can fund an HSA. In 2019, the contribution limits to an HSA are as follows:

- $3,500 for individual coverage
- $7,000 for family coverage
- $1,000 catch-up contribution for those 55 or older

Now at this point you may be wondering why I'm talking about HSAs in a chapter on retirement accounts. Great question. There are two reasons.

First, the tax advantages of an HSA are without equal. Imagine taking the tax deductibility of a Traditional 401(k) and combining it with the tax-free withdrawals of a Roth 401(k). With an HSA, you get three tax advantages:

1. Contributions are tax deductible, regardless of your income;
2. The account grows tax-deferred; and
3. Distributions from the account are tax-free, so long as they are used for qualified medical expenses.

This is true regardless of when you use the money. You don't have to wait until you are a certain age. HSAs are a beautiful thing.

Second, HSAs can be used for retirement savings. Unlike a Flexible Spending Account, you don't have to use the money in an HSA in the year you make the contribution or risk losing it. In fact, you can leave the money in an HSA for decades. Then once you reach retirement, you can use the money for health expenses without paying a nickel in taxes.

There's an added benefit. You can use HSA funds for nonmedical expenses. If you do, you lose the third tax advantage. The distribution is treated as ordinary income for taxes purposes. And, if you have not reached age 65, the distribution is subject to a 20% penalty tax. Once you reach 65, however, the 20% penalty goes away.

Advanced Tip: Imagine you spend $1,000 on qualified medical expenses this year. While you could pay for this expense from your HSA, let's assume you decide to leave the money in the HSA for retirement and pay the bill from your checking account. Save the receipt. You can withdraw money from an HSA for qualified medical expenses that you incurred years earlier. You could wait 30 years with that $1,000 receipt in a shoe box, and then use it to take out $1,000 tax and penalty free from your HSA, so long as you incurred the medical expense after you established your HSA account.

The Plan

Now that we understand workplace retirement plans, IRAs, the Roth versions of both, and HSAs, it's time to walk through the Plan. What follows is the order of account types in which I believe most people should invest their money. There are exceptions, of course, which we'll cover shortly.

Step #1 Contribute enough to your Roth 401(k) to get the company match.

Step #2 Max out your Roth IRA.

Step #3 Max out an HSA (Health Savings Account) if you have a qualifying HDHP.

Step #4 Finish contributing the maximum to your Roth 401(k).

Step #5 Invest the remainder in a taxable account.

The Details

Step #1: Contribute enough to your Roth 401(k) to get the company match.

The first step is to contribute enough to a Roth 401(k) to take full advantage of your employer's matching contributions. This is typically three to six percent of your income up to a certain limit. If your employer doesn't offer a Roth, then contribute to a Traditional 401(k) to take full advantage of any company match. Why do we start here? Several reasons.

First, if your employer matches your contributions, it's critical you take full advantage of the match. Failing to do so is like having a winning lottery ticket and setting it on fire.

AGTM: Always Get the Match.

Let's put this into perspective by returning to our hypothetical:

- Annual Income: $75,000
- Saving Rate: 20% ($15,000 a year)
- Spending Rate: 80% ($60,000 a year)
- Return: 9.3%

Now let's also assume our employer matches 401(k) contributions dollar for dollar, up to 6% of our salary. That means we can add $4,500, or nearly one-third, to the amount we save, simply by contributing to the 401(k).

And the employer match reduces our time to get to Level 7 by more than three years.

Yeah, take the match.

Factoid: All employer matching contributions are made to a Traditional 401(k), not a Roth 401(k). This is true even if *your* contributions are to a Roth 401(k). The reason is that employer matching contributions are not added to your taxable income. Thus, if you contribute to a Roth 401(k) and have employer matching contributions, you'll in effect have two 401(k) accounts—one a Roth and one a Traditional 401(k).

The second reason I like prioritizing 401(k) contributions is that the employer makes the contribution for you. You decide which investment options you want and the amount to contribute, but your employer deducts the money from your paycheck automatically and deposits the money into your 401(k). This automation enables you to save without ever touching the money.

Step #2: Max out your Roth IRA.

The next step is to max out your Roth IRA. You are saving a lot of money if you get this far. You've put thousands of dollars away in a Roth 401(k). And now you are saving $6,000 more in a Roth IRA. Some of you won't have that much to save. That's ok. But if you do, the Roth IRA is next up.

- If your income disqualifies you from contributing to a Roth IRA, use the Backdoor Roth IRA.

Step #3: Max out an HSA (Health Savings Account) if you have a qualifying HDHP.

Once you've taken advantage of your employer's matching contributions and funded a Roth IRA, turn to funding an HSA if you have a qualifying HDHP. The tax benefits are just too good to pass up. In addition, many employers fund a portion of the HSA for you.

Here I should say that some would argue you should fund an HSA before a Roth IRA. Frankly, it's a close call. I prefer funding a Roth IRA first for two reasons: (1) Contributions can be withdrawn at any time without tax or penalty, and (2) distributions from an HSA incur a 20% penalty if they are not for qualified medical expenses and occur before the age of 65.

Step #4: Finish contributing the maximum to your Roth 401(k).

Step #1 is to contribute enough to your Roth 401(k) to get the match. It's here that we finish maxing out our 401(k).

Step #5: Invest the remainder in a taxable account.

Once you've maxed out all of your available tax advantage accounts, a taxable account is last in line.

The Exceptions

I believe the above plan is an ideal approach for most people. There are, however, exceptions.

High Taxes

Those in the top tax brackets may be better off avoiding Roth retirement accounts. The reason is that the higher your tax bracket, the more valuable the tax deductions from making contributions to traditional retirement accounts. Here it's important to consider both state and federal taxes.

Imagine your income puts you in the 37% federal tax bracket and the 13.3% California tax bracket. (Yep, those on the West Coast pay a lot in taxes). You have a combined marginal tax rate of 50.3%. In such cases, I'd contribute to traditional retirement accounts because the deduction would be worth 50 cents for every $1 invested.

Compare the above to somebody living in Tennessee in the 20% federal tax bracket. They pay no income tax in Tennessee. A Roth retirement account is a no-brainer.

Horrible Investment Options

Recall that with workplace retirement accounts, you must select from the available investment choices offered by your employer's plan. In some cases, you may find that all of your options are horrible. And by horrible, I mean very expensive (see the chapter on fees). This is becoming less common, but it's still possible.

In such cases, I'd contribute enough to get the match, but no more. When you leave your job, you can roll your 401(k) investments into either an IRA or the workplace retirement plan at your new employer.

Health Issues

The above plan assumes that HSA contributions will be saved for retirement, and not to pay your current medical bills. Health issues, however, may necessitate that you prioritize HSA contributions. If you know you're going to have significant medical bills and you can't max out all of your retirement accounts, funding an HSA should be a priority. It's still important to contribute enough to a 401(k) to get the match, if you can. But you may need to make HSA contributions your top financial priority.

Multitask

The above plan is described step-by-step. Partially fund a Roth 401(k), then a Roth IRA, then an HSA, and so on. But life isn't always that simple. As I noted above, you may need to make HSA contributions more of a priority. In addition, you may choose to split your money across several accounts at the same time. That's perfectly fine. The key is to keep an eye on (1) employer matching opportunities to 401(k) and HSA accounts, (2) your medical needs, and (3) the benefits of a Roth IRA as an emergency fund (you can easily take out your contributions—not your earnings—tax and penalty free at any time).

Very Early Retirement

For those who want to retire long before age 60, additional considerations come into play.

First, you must think about how you'll access your retirement accounts. That's particularly true with HSAs. Until the age of 65, you can't take money out of an HSA for nonmedical reasons without paying taxes and a 20% penalty. In many cases this isn't much of an issue, as the money in your retirement and taxable accounts can fund your living expenses. Still, you may need to curtail HSA contributions if your other accounts can't handle your early retirement needs until you turn 65.

Second, extreme early retirement may influence your decision between Roth and traditional retirement accounts. One approach is to contribute to traditional retirement accounts during your working years even if you are in a lower income tax bracket. Once you retire and your taxable income goes to near $0, you can start converting your traditional retirement accounts to a Roth IRA. These conversions will be treated as taxable income in the year you execute the conversion. So long as you don't convert too much in one year, however, you can keep your taxable income very low.

This strategy is called a **Roth IRA Conversion Ladder**. Roth conversions come with their own set of unique rules and considerations. If this is of interest to you, here are some excellent resources for additional reading:

- How to Create a Roth IRA Conversion Ladder (MoneyUnder30): https://www.moneyunder30.com/roth-ira-conversion-ladder
- How to Access Retirement Funds Early (MadFientist): https://www.madfientist.com/how-to-access-retirement-funds-early
- Roth IRA Conversion Calculator (Schwab): https://www.schwab.com/public/schwab/investing/retirement_and_planning/understanding_iras/ira_calculators/roth_ira_conversion
- Tax-Savvy Roth IRA Conversions (Fidelity): https://www.fidelity.com/viewpoints/retirement/tax-savvy-roth-conversions

Emergency Savings

One thing we haven't covered is emergency savings. Here I'm talking about money you can use when your car breaks down, your roof leaks, or you lose your job. We need to answer three questions:

1. How much should we save for emergencies?
2. Where should we keep our emergency fund?
3. Where should it fit with our other financial goals?

While there is no one "right" answer, I believe the following is a reasonable plan of action:

- Save one month of expenses before anything else. This takes priority over retirement savings.
- Keep your emergency fund in a high yield online savings account. They pay the best rates and separating your emergency fund from your checking account protects it from moments where you may be tempted to spend it.
- Once you have one month of expenses saved, begin working towards contributing enough to your 401(k) to get the employer match, if any.
- Once you've got the match, look to fund your Roth IRA. As noted above, you can always withdraw your contributions from a Roth IRA tax and penalty free. In this regard, a Roth IRA can be used for true emergencies.

3 KEY CONCEPTS

1. Retirement accounts can speed our journey to Level 7 by minimizing our tax liability.

2. Roth retirement accounts are the better option for most people.

3. HSA accounts offer the single best tax-advantaged account available today and can be used for retirement with proper planning.

CHAPTER 24

How to Evaluate a Mutual Fund

I magine you're psyched to get started investing. You are a Freedom Fighter, after all. You've decided to start contributing to your company's Roth 401(k). You're excited about the company match and how easy it is to invest (having read this far in the book). With your heart racing, you log into your company's 401(k), and like air being let out of a balloon, your excitement gives way to fear.

If your 401(k) is anything like mine, it can be intimidating. My current employer runs its 401(k) through Fidelity. In my account, I see 29 investment options.

Here's what the first few look like:

Name/Inception Date	Asset Class	1 Year	3 Year	5 Year	10 Year/ LOF*
AF GRTH FUND AMER R6 (RGAGX)	Stock Investments	6.92%	12.73%	11.63%	14.96%
FID 500 INDEX (FXAIX)	Stock Investments	6.26%	12.15%	11.11%	14.31%
FID CONTRAFUND K (FCNKX)	Stock Investments	6.62%	12.82%	11.76%	15.14%
FID DIVERSIFD INTL K (FDIKX)	Stock Investments	-9.15%	2.73%	2.41%	8.36%

Now what do we do? When I first started to invest, I did what many people do. I looked at past performance. Why not pick the funds with the best track record? That approach led to more questions. Do I use the past year's performance, past three years, five years, 10 years? And what if the funds I pick don't do as well going forward as they have in the past? Help!

Don't worry. You've got this. In this chapter we are going to walk through how to evaluate a mutual fund. We'll use my 401(k) options as an example. You'll learn how to evaluate these funds to pick either a Target Date Retirement fund or build a 3-Fund Portfolio. Armed with this information, you'll be able to do the same with your 401(k).

The only tool we'll be using is Morningstar.com. All of the information we'll need is available for free from Morningstar. It's also available for free from your 401(k). Because different 401(k) plans provide this information in different ways, however, I've used Morningstar throughout this chapter. In the video at the end of the chapter, however, I also show you how this information appears in my 401(k) with Fidelity.

Target Date Retirement Funds

I like to start with TDRs. It's easy to tell if your 401(k) offers them. The mutual fund names have years in them. My 401(k) offers what Fidelity calls Freedom Funds. Freedom Fund is the name Fidelity has given to its TDRs. For our purposes, let's evaluate the "Fid Freedom 2040 K (FSNVX)" fund.

Now, what do we need to know about this fund? With TDRs, we need to know just two things:

- Fees
- Stock/Bond Allocation

We can get all of this information from Morningstar. Navigate to Morningstar.com and you'll see a box at the top to enter the ticker symbol. In this case, enter FSNVX for the Fidelity 2040 Freedom Fund. You'll see a page with summary information on the fund.

First, let's examine the fees. Here, you'll find what you need near the top of the page under two headings: Load and Expenses. Load tells us if there are any Load fees. For this fund there is none. Excellent. Expenses tell us what the

Expense Ratio is. For FSNVX, the expense ratio is 0.65%. Not so excellent.

Sixty-five basis points is just too much. We want to get to Level 7 as quickly as possible. If we could save, for example, 50 basis points in expenses by finding funds that charge 15 basis points or less, we can shave 12 months or more off the time it takes us to get to Level 7. And that's for doing nothing except picking the right mutual fund.

Given the fees, we could stop here and move to examine the 3-Fund Portfolio. But let's continue in case: (1) you have a TDR option that costs less, (2) an expensive TDR is your best available option, or (3) you've decided to stick with a TDR because of its convenience.

So let's now look at the stock/bond allocation. In most cases, TDRs have a reasonable stock/bond allocation given your years to retirement. To get this information, simply click the "Portfolio" link near the top of the page. According to Morningstar, Fidelity's 2040 Freedom Fund has the following stock/bond allocation:

Stocks: 85%
Bonds: 15% (including cash)

For somebody planning to retire in 2040, an 85/15 stock/bond allocation is reasonable.

Tip: You don't have to pick the TDR that corresponds to when you plan to retire. Even if you plan to retire in 2040, you could still invest in a 2050 fund, for example. The TDR police won't arrest you, I promise. Why might we do this? To get the stock/bond allocation that you want. For example, if you wanted a 90/10 stock to bond allocation, you could find the TDR available in your 401(k) that offered a 90/10 allocation. It doesn't matter that the fund's name includes a year that doesn't correspond with your planned retirement date. You would, however, want to keep an eye on the allocation as it changes over time to make sure it aligns with your investment goals.

3-Fund Portfolio

Recall that for our 3-Fund Portfolio, we need just three index funds:

- U.S. stock fund
- U.S. bond fund
- International stock fund

Returning to my 401(k) and its list of funds, we can see an "FID 500 Index (FXAIX)" fund. The name suggests that this fund is an S&P 500 index fund, but we should make sure. Searching its ticker in Morningstar, we see that it is. From Morningstar we learn the following:

- The fund's full name is the Fidelity 500 Index Fund.
- It charges no Load Fees.
- Its Expense Ratio is just 0.02%.
- It tracks the S&P 500 index.

In short, FXAIX is perfect for the U.S. stock fund component of a 3-Fund Portfolio.

Next we need a bond fund. Here the "FID US BOND IDX (FXNAX)" fund jumps out at us. Does "IDX" stand for index? Let's find out. Searching the ticker in Morningstar reveals that FXNAX is the Fidelity Bond Index Fund. It charges just 3 basis points in fees, no load fee, and invests in intermediate-term mostly U.S. bonds. A quick visit to the "Portfolio" link reveals that more than 90% of the fund is invested in U.S. bonds. Perfect. Let's add it to our 3-Fund Portfolio.

Now all we need is a total international stock fund. A quick scan of our available funds reveals the "FID INTL INDEX (FSPSX)" fund. Morningstar tells us this fund charges just five basis points in fees and invests in a blend (both growth and value) of large foreign based companies. We can jump to the "Portfolio" tab to learn more about the fund's investments. Here we learn, for example, how much of the fund is invested in the Americas, Europe, and Asia.

And there you have it. A perfect 3-Fund Portfolio based on low cost Fidelity funds. And you can follow the same process to find emerging market funds, small cap funds, REITs, or anything else your 401(k) may offer.

3 KEY CONCEPTS

1. Evaluating mutual funds is easier than many people think.

2. Using free tools such as Morningstar, you can quickly evaluate any mutual fund in your 401(k).

3. With this evaluation method, it's easy to find a TDR or build a 3-Fund Portfolio.

Video: https://www.retirebeforemomanddad.com/Chapter24

CHAPTER 25

Let's Do This

"The best time to plant a tree is twenty years ago. The second best time is now."

– Unknown

We now have all the tools we need to make our first investment. We know from the previous chapters where to start. If you have a 401(k), that's where you start. If not, open a Roth IRA and consider an HSA if you have a HDHP.

"But how do I do this?" you ask. Good question. That's what this chapter answers. First, we'll look at getting started with workplace retirement plans, like a 401(k). Then we'll turn to IRAs and taxable accounts.

> **Note about HSAs**: If you have an HDHP, your employer will work with a company to manage your HSA. Many employers contribute to your HSA as well. HSA accounts typically have several investment options to consider, similar to a 401(k). We'll focus on 401(k) accounts in this chapter, but the guidance applies to HSA accounts as well.

Workplace Retirement Plans

Getting started with a 401(k) has some advantages. You don't have to decide where to open the account. Your employer has already set it up. You have the folks in HR to help you if you have questions. And the 401(k) plan administrators have help lines you can call.

If you don't know how to sign up for your 401(k), contact HR. They will tell you how to get started. Do it now. I'll wait.

Good. So now we have to decide two things:

1. How much are we going to invest?
2. What are we going to invest in?

From previous chapters, you should already know what percentage of your gross income you plan to save. For many of you, this amount will be less than the contribution limit of a 401(k). You can set your contributions to a 401(k) as a percentage of your salary. It couldn't be any easier.

Now, what are we going to invest in? From previous chapters, you already know about Target Date Retirement (TDR) funds. That's a good place to start. First, we need to do some legwork.

Most 401(k)s today offer TDR funds. Find the TDR fund in your 401(k) that corresponds to the year you want to retire. It doesn't have to be the exact year. Remember, TDRs come in five-year increments. Just find the closest one.

Now use what you learned in the last chapter to evaluate the fund's expenses and asset allocation. Take the fund's ticker symbol and search for the fund in Morningstar.com. Once you find it, the Expense Ratio will be near the top of the page under the heading "Expenses." It's that simple.

As we discussed, 401(k) and other workplace retirement plans come with a set list of investments for you to choose. You are limited to that list, in most cases.[35] So why bother looking at the Expense Ratio? It's not like you can order something that's not on the menu.

---

35 Some 401(k) plans do enable employees to invest through a brokerage account that opens up many new investment options. If your 401(k) doesn't offer excellent mutual fund options, see if a brokerage window, as some call it, is available.

Two reasons. First, you should develop the habit of understanding the costs of any investment you entrust your hard-earned money to. Would you buy a TV without knowing the cost?

Second, if the cost of a TDR is above 25 basis points (0.25%), it's too expensive. I'd prefer to see the Expense Ratio below 15 basis points. Anything above 100 basis points (1%) is highway robbery. If your company doesn't offer TDR fund options for 25 basis points or less, you should do two things.

First, evaluate the other fund options for lower cost index funds. You can build the 3-Fund Portfolio very easily, as we walked through in the last chapter. You may find a U.S. stock index fund, international stock index fund, and U.S. bond index fund for considerably less cost than the TDR options in your 401(k).

Second, talk to HR about getting lower cost mutual fund options. You won't get results immediately. But if enough employees raise this issue, eventually you may see a change for the better.

And that's it. In a matter of minutes you've become an investor. You've signed up for your company's 401(k). You've decided how much to contribute. You've selected your investments. You're on your way.

IRAs

A 401(k) is a lot like a buffet. You get a lot of choices but only the choices the restaurant decides to put out on the table. Take as much as you want from what is offered, but don't expect to order something that's not part of the buffet. On top of that, the 401(k) decides which buffet you'll order from.

With an IRA, you pick the restaurant and you order whatever you want. You get to find low cost investments that appeal to you. That's also, in a way, the bad news. *You* have to decide. You have to choose.

The first step is to decide where you want to open your IRA. My choice has always been Vanguard. They have a large selection of low-cost index funds. They don't charge account fees to open an IRA. Their website is easy to navigate.

There are, of course, other options. Here's a list of alternatives that I think are reasonable choices:

- **Fidelity** offers several index funds at very low cost. And recently it introduced some index funds that have no costs. Its TDR funds are on the expensive side, so I'd avoid them. If you want a TDR fund, Fidelity is not your best choice. There is no minimum investment required to open an IRA at Fidelity, but some mutual funds do have minimum investment requirements.

- **Schwab** surprised me with its low-cost funds. I expected Schwab to be expensive, but my research found the opposite. It offers TDR funds for just eight basis points. Many of its index funds cost less than five basis points. Its minimum deposit for an IRA is $1,000.

- **Betterment** is a type of investment company commonly called a robo-advisor. Betterment offers tools that make it incredibly easy to create a diversified stock and bond portfolio. It's similar in concept to a Target Date Retirement fund, but it gives you more flexibility when it comes to your stock/bond allocation. It does come with a fee, so it's not the least expensive option. I do think, however, that it is a reasonable choice.

> **Resource**: There are a number of robo-advisor options similar to Betterment. You can find an updated list of alternatives at https://www.retirebeforemomanddad.com/Resources.

Once you've selected where to open an IRA, it's just a matter of doing it. You can open most IRAs online. If you encounter any problems, simply call the company. I've found Vanguard and Fidelity, for example, to be incredibly easy to work with.

Once your account is open, you can make an initial investment into a TDR fund or other index funds. You can set up automatic monthly transfers from your checking account. Alternatively, you can fund your IRA periodically throughout the year or just once. Just remember not to contribute more than what is permitted by the IRS.

Taxable Accounts

Opening a taxable account is not much different than opening an IRA. We keep our taxable accounts with the same company that has our IRAs. It keeps things simple.

You open a taxable account pretty much the same way as you open an IRA. There are a few differences, of course. The primary difference is that there is no limitation to the amount you can contribute to a taxable account. With a taxable account, you don't have to decide between a Traditional and Roth account. And there will be different forms to complete for a taxable account than for an IRA. The information you need, however, is pretty much the same.

Beyond that, the process is nearly identical.

Welcome to the world of investing. Simple. Easy. Awesome.

In the next chapter we turn to what is without a doubt the biggest threat to your investments. You!

3 KEY CONCEPTS

1. Just do it.

2. Just do it.

3. Just do it.

CHAPTER 26

You

"It's one thing to shoot yourself in the foot. Just don't reload the gun."
– Senator Lindsey Graham

We've come a long way. We've learned about the Money Multiplier and how it can propel us on our journey to Financial Freedom. We've learned the importance of our Savings and Spending Rates. We have strategies regarding how to increase our Saving Rate. And we know how to invest.

Now imagine that you take what you've learned to open an IRA or start investing in a 401(k) or both. As we've discussed, you start evaluating a mutual fund. Let's imagine you are looking at the Fidelity New Millennium Fund (FMILX). It was named one of the top 25 mutual funds by Kiplinger in 2018. So let's review how we might evaluate this fund.

First, we enter the ticker symbol (FMILX) into Morningstar. The first thing we note is that it has an Expense Ratio of 53 basis points. Not as low as we'd like but not awful. Of course, we don't even know what FMILX invests in. Is it a stock or bond fund, U.S. or international, large cap or small cap?

Fortunately, Morningstar gives us the answer. We learn from the "Asset Allocation" box when we search the ticker in Morningstar that the fund holds just over 82% of its assets in U.S. stocks and about 15% in non-U.S. stocks. We also know from what Morningstar calls the "Style Map" that the fund invests in large companies.

So far, so good. Now we want to understand the fund's past performance.

We have heard that "past performance is no guarantee of future results." Yet as Mark Twain said, "history doesn't repeat itself but it often rhymes."

So you look at the fund's past performance and see that it has averaged a 14.18%[36] return over the past decade. Not bad. The S&P 500 returned about 13.24% over the same period. So FMILX beat the index by nearly 1% after fees. That's not easy to do over a 10-year period.

Then you notice something curious. While the Total Returns were 14.18% according to Morningstar, there's a link to something called "Investor Returns." Why would that be different than Total Returns, you wonder. So you click on the link.

It turns out that while the fund has averaged a 14.18% return over the past decade; Investor Returns, whatever that means, came in at just 13.09%. That's less than the 13.24% of the S&P 500 and more than 100 basis points lower than Total Returns. What? How can that be?

Investor Returns represents Morningstar's analysis of the average return earned by investors in the mutual fund. Why would it be different than Total Returns?

Total Returns represents the return earned by the fund assuming we invest a lump sum at the beginning of the time period and leave it there untouched, in this case for 10 years. The Total Return assumes that no additional funds are invested during the time period and that no funds are withdrawn.

In real life, however, things aren't so simple. Investors tend to get excited when the market is up and scared when it's down. They invest more when they are excited and take money out when they are nervous. The result is almost always the same—investors underperform the fund's Total Return because they are terrible at timing the market.

Welcome to the biggest threat to your journey to Financial Freedom—you.

When I talk to people who have never invested, I find they are often intimidated. They are not sure how to get started. They don't know what to invest in. Should they invest in a 401(k) or an IRA? Roth or Traditional? How much should they put in stocks versus bonds? We've covered all of these questions,

---

36 *As of 10/31/2018, as are the other returns data in this chapter.*

and they are important. But as I hope you now know, there was nothing to be intimidated by. All this stuff is the easy part.

The hard part isn't coming up with a plan. The hard part is sticking to it. As boxing champ Mike Tyson says, "Everybody has a plan until they get punched in the mouth." As investors, we get punched in the mouth. A lot.

And the punches don't just come from the stock market. Think back to the 2008-2009 market crash. From October 2007 to March 2009, the S&P 500 index lost 56.4%. More than half its pre-crash value evaporated in 18 months. Poof. Gone.

And that's the good news. A lot of other train wrecks were occurring:

- The banking industry was teetering on the brink of collapse.
- So was the auto industry.
- Home values plummeted.
- Home foreclosures spiked.
- The unemployment rate jumped, hitting 10% in October 2009.

Our economy was in trouble and people were scared. Yet as bad as things were, let's put 2007-2009 into perspective. The stock market has seen some really tough times:

- The stock market crash of 1929
- The Great Depression
- WWII
- The Korean War
- The Bay of Pigs and the Cuban Missile Crisis
- The Vietnam War
- The Oil Embargo
- Interest rates near 20% (1980-1982)
- Black Monday (1987—market crashes 22.6% in one day)
- Dot-Com Bubble
- 9/11

Here's the point. We don't know what the next crisis will be. We also don't know when it will occur. But we know one thing for sure. There will be a next one. And a next one. And a next one.

So how do we prepare mentally and emotionally to stand our ground during the next stock market free-fall?

Expectations

First, we need to set realistic expectations. If we expect the markets to go up each year by 10%, we are in for a big disappointment. Sometimes the markets fall fast. We need to expect that some years and maybe even some decades won't see market gains.

Having the right expectation isn't enough. But it's a start. In the words of author M. Scott Peck:

"Life is difficult. This is a great truth, one of the greatest truths. It is a great truth because once we truly see this truth, we transcend it. Once we truly know that life is difficult—once we truly understand and accept it—then life is no longer difficult. Because once it is accepted, the fact that life is difficult no longer matters."

Sticking to an investment plan is difficult.

History

Part of setting the right expectations is understanding the history of the stock market. As discussed above, the stock market has seen some dark days. And there will always be dark days ahead. But there are also sunny days.

Remember the more than 50% drop in the market from 2007 to 2009? I've talked to many people who, in fear, sold some or even all of their investments during that time. They tell me their stories today with profound regret. Why?

Because the dark days of 2007-2009 were followed by a lot of sunshine. By 2012, the stock market losses had been erased. The market had fully recovered. And if you had continued to invest during those dark days, you did even better. You were buying while the prices were low, and then reaping the benefits as the market recovered.

In fact, the decade since 2009 has seen some of the best market returns in history. Here are the returns of the S&P 500 beginning in 2007:[37]

2007	3.53%
2008	38.49%
2009	23.45%
2010	12.78%
2011	0.00%
2012	13.41%
2013	29.60%
2014	11.39%
2015	-0.73%
2016	9.54%
2017	19.42%
2018	-6.24%

It's interesting that 2009 saw an increase of 23.45%. Remember that from late 2007 to March 2009, the market had dropped by more than 50%. But by the end of 2009 it had gone up, ending the year with a gain of over 23%.

And here's the thing: The above returns are "normal." What I mean is that good years often follow bad years. And bad years often follow good years.

For example, following four very rough years beginning in 1929, the market was up 46% in 1933 and 41% in 1935. In 1937 the market was down more than 38%, yet it was up more than 25% in both the year before and the year after.

More recent years are no different. In 1974, the market was down almost 30%, yet it was up more than 31% the next year and more than 19% the year after that. When the tech bubble burst, stocks were down double-digits for three years in a row beginning in 2000. It followed, however, with an up year of more than 26% in 2003. And since 2004, the market has been up every year

37 https://www.macrotrends.net/2526/sp-500-historical-annual-returns

but four.

None of this fluctuation surprises those who know the history of the stock market. Don't let it surprise you either.

The Value of a Falling Market

The third thing to understand is that there is tremendous value to most investors in a falling market. The value comes in three ways.

First, as you make monthly or yearly investments in your 401(k), IRA, and taxable accounts, the lower the price the better. You'd much rather buy into an S&P 500 index fund at say $100 a share than $200, right? When the market goes down, the shares of the mutual funds you invest in also go down. Your regular investments buy more shares.

Think back to 2008. The S&P 500 index was down over 38%. That means investments in an S&P 500 index fund you made at the end of 2008 were 38% cheaper than at the beginning of the year. Had the market stayed flat that year, you would have been worse off. Instead, the market went down, investors got more shares for each invested dollar, and in the long run, they were better off.

Second, most mutual funds pay dividends. The Vanguard Total International Stock Index Fund (VTIAX) for example, has a dividend yield of just over 3%. You can get this information from Vanguard or from Morningstar and other online financial websites.

Most investors have the dividend automatically reinvested back into the mutual fund. When this happens, the dividend is used to purchase new shares at the current price. Just like making new investments, reinvesting dividends at lower prices is a boon for long-term investors.

Finally, many companies repurchase their own shares from the public. When they do this, remaining shareholders own more of the company because there are fewer outstanding shares. It's like owning the same piece of pie you've always owned, but the total pie got smaller.

As an investor, I want the company to spend as little money as possible to get the most shares. This only happens when the share price is down. Thus, investors are better off when companies repurchase their own shares at rock bottom prices, as in 2008 and 2009.

In other words, low stock prices benefit long-term investors.

Now, I don't pretend that the above will make the next market crash a walk in the park. It won't. But you should take comfort that for long-term buy and hold investors, market crashes make us richer *if,* and only if, we stick to our investment plan.

The Right Asset Allocation

As you know, Asset Allocation refers to the mix of stock and bond funds in our portfolio. The most important decision you'll make when it comes to Asset Allocation is how much money to invest in bond funds and how much in stock funds. We've used a 70% stock fund and 30% bond fund Asset Allocation as an example throughout this book. But a 70/30 portfolio is not the only reasonable choice.

So what does this have to do with surviving a market crash? I'm glad you asked. Conventional wisdom says that if you fear stock market drops, you should have a more conservative portfolio. And by conservative, we mean that you should have more in bonds than a person who may not fear a stock market drop as much as you do.

While I take no issue with this concept in general, it does have a few problems.

First, we need to reach our financial goals. To do that, we need a certain return on our investments over time. While a conservative portfolio may address your fear of the stock market, it may cause you to miss the goals that prompted you to invest in the first place.

Second, when you are just starting out, it's hard to know how you'll feel in a bear market. Surely none of us likes to see the value of our portfolio plummet. But exactly how would you handle 2007-2009 if you had never lived through that type of market before?

Third, even if you have lived through a bear market, that doesn't mean you'll react the same way in the next bear market. By then you'll likely (1) have more money in the market, and (2) be closer to retirement or at least Financial Freedom. These factors can change the way we react during bad times. We may have been just fine riding out a bad market with $50,000 in a 401(k) and a couple of decades before Level 7. Will you react the same way with $1 million in the market and just three years from Level 7?

So what does this mean? It means that you certainly can adjust your stock/bond allocation based on your fear of market fluctuations. But don't expect this one factor to address all of your concerns. It won't.

And that brings me to the next consideration.

Debt

What so many experts miss is the importance of our overall financial picture when it comes to surviving a bad market. Nobody likes to see the market fall by 10, 20, or 30%. But it's a lot easier to handle when your financial house is in order.

The key here is debt. By keeping your debt burden low, you position yourself to handle just about any market. But what is a "low" debt burden?

We'll talk more about debt in the next section of the book. For now, here are a few rules of thumb.

First, avoid lifestyle debt like the plague. This is debt we incur, usually on a credit card, to fund our living expenses. Often credit cards fund spending we could avoid, like eating out, vacations, and so on. Sometimes credit cards fund necessities, particularly if you experience a prolonged job loss.

I don't pretend it's always easy. But do everything in your power to avoid paying for living expenses on credit. It's the worst possible debt because you have nothing of lasting value to show for the debt you've incurred. (You can't return the vacation you just took or the meal you just ate).

Second, work hard to avoid car loans. We've already discussed how the cost of a car, even if we pay cash, affects our journey to Level 7. Add in debt with interest, and the problem gets worse. If you do decide to finance a car purchase, get the least expensive car possible. Remember, we buy our Financial Freedom first. Then you can get a nice car if that's what you choose.

Third, be smart about your student debt. There are ways to keep your debt burden to a minimum, including loan forgiveness programs, various debt repayment plans, and even refinancing student loans to a lower interest rate. By keeping your monthly obligations to a reasonable amount given your income, you take pressure off your monthly budget. This in turn enables you to save more, and it gives you some breathing room during bad financial times.

Finally, don't be house poor. Buying a home is one of the few instances when taking on some debt is a reasonable choice. But too much of a good thing becomes a really bad thing. It's kind of like the third piece of chocolate cake. The first one? Maybe. The third one? I don't think so.

Here, a good rule of thumb is to spend no more than 20% of your monthly gross income on housing expenses. I understand that in some areas of the country this may be unrealistic. But I've found that as you spend more than that, your housing costs start to cause you problems in other areas of your financial life.

Whatever specific choices you make, remember that your debt levels have a big effect on your ability to handle a falling stock market.

Never Stop Learning

Last, never stop learning about investing and finances. I've been at this for 30+ years and I learn new things all the time. Read the Wall Street Journal, even once a week. Read a good book on investing, even just one a year.

You don't have to be a money geek like I am. But don't stick your head in the sand either.

3 KEY CONCEPTS

1. The biggest risk in our journey to Level 7 is our own fear and greed. Both can cause us to make investment mistakes.

2. The key is to stick to our investment plan through good markets and bad.

3. To help yourself do this, never stop learning.

CHAPTER 27

Getting Investment Help

"Those who are happiest are those who do the most for others."
– Booker T. Washington

W hat if you want help?
I've been a DIY investor for nearly 30 years. I can't imagine turning my portfolio over to somebody else to manage. I do understand, however, that not everybody wants to manage their investments. If this is the case for you, the good news is that you have low-cost options.

Here we need to better understand how investment professionals charge fees. This falls into two categories: Commissions and fee-only. Let's look at both.

Commissions

Some investment professionals earn fees through commissions paid to them from the investments they sell you. That's the purpose of the Load Fee that some mutual fund companies charge, and a portion of it goes to the investment broker. The same is true for expensive insurance products, like indexed annuities, that many commissioned brokers try to push on unsuspecting victims (I guess you know where I stand on indexed annuities).

One criticism of this fee structure is the potential for conflicts of interest. By earning their fee through commissions, these investment professionals have a powerful incentive to sell you only investments that pay them a fee. They will almost never recommend, for example, a low-cost index fund. Why? They can't earn a fee from the sale.

The solution, in theory, is to hire an investment professional who charges you directly for their services. Enter the *fee-only* investment advisor.

Fee-Only

With a fee-only advisor, the potential for a conflict of interest is diminished, at least in theory. Since they don't get paid based on the investments they sell you, their only motivation is to put you in the best investment possible.

That's not to say conflicts are impossible. Most fee-only advisors are paid a percentage of the amount of money you invest with them. Now imagine asking a fee-only advisor whether you should pay off your mortgage or take the money and invest it with them? A potential conflict arises. But I digress.

Back to the fees. The problem with a fee-only advisor is that their fees are often outrageous. And it gets worse. The fees don't *seem* outrageous. The industry standard is 1% of Assets Under Management (AUM). That's a fancy way of saying how much money you invest with them.

At 1%, you'll pay $1,000 a year for every $100,000 you invest. I'm sure that by now you know a 1% fee will wreck your Freedom Fund. It will lengthen your journey to Level 7 by two to three years, and it could cost you hundreds of thousands of dollars over your lifetime.

And in retirement it gets worse. Recall that we can take out about 4% of our investments in year one. How does that change if we have to give 1% to an investment advisor? Our $40,000 on a $1 million nest egg just turned into $30,000.

Low Cost Options

There is good news. There are some fee-only investment advisors who charge far less than 1%. If you are looking for help, below are some recommendations.

(Disclosure: I have NO financial incentive to recommend any of these individuals or companies.)

1. **Vanguard**: With investments of $50,000 or more, Vanguard will manage your portfolio for 30 basis points. This is in addition to the cost of the mutual funds. Since they are primarily index funds, the Expense Ratios of the funds are extremely low.

2. **PlanVision**: I've worked with Mark Zoril of PlanVision for a couple of years now. He was also a guest on my podcast. He charges—are you ready for this?—$96 a year. That's it. He doesn't manage your investments for you, but he will help you build a solid portfolio. He'll also help you with everything from a budget to retirement projections to insurance to social security. You can get more information on PlanVision here: https://planvisionmn.com/.

3. **Robo-Advisors**: As we discussed earlier, services such as Betterment offer low cost tools to help you build a solid portfolio. They use automation to help investors build low-cost, diversified portfolios using index ETFs (an ETF is similar to a mutual fund, but it trades like a stock). The typical fee is about 25 to 35 basis points. Some services also provide an advisor you can talk to about your portfolio, although in that case the fee will likely be higher.

3 KEY CONCEPTS

1. The best option is to handle your own investments. If you want help, however, you must consider the cost.

2. Traditional commissioned and even fee-only advisors are just too expensive for Freedom Fighters.

3. There are, however, several options that provide excellent services at a reasonable cost.

Part 5

Practical Considerations

CHAPTER 28

The Progress Principle

"Great things are done by a series of small things brought together."
– Vincent Van Gogh

We started our journey trying to imagine what it would be like to be a millionaire on a $50,000 a year salary. Recall that we assumed no raises and that we could only save 5% of our income. Yet the results were surprising, to say the least. After 45 years, we had accumulated over $1.7 million.

It's a perfect example of how relatively small steps, taken consistently over time, enable us to accomplish big goals. The same is true when it comes to your Saving Rate.

By now you know that saving 20% of your income enables you to reach Level 7 Financial Freedom in about 31 years. Save 30% and you reach Level 7 in about 25 years. Yet just like our goal of becoming a millionaire on a $50,000 a year salary with no raises, saving 20 or 30% of your income may seem impossible to you. Maybe it IS impossible right now.

We can apply the principle of small steps to our Saving Rate. It's great if you can save 30% or more of your income today to put towards your freedom. But if you can't, it's not the end of your Financial Freedom journey. It's the beginning.

It's here that I want to introduce you to a concept called The Progress Principle. About 10 years ago I attended a blogging conference in Las Vegas with a group of financial bloggers. At the conference we had lunch and discussed our business goals. Most of us, myself included, had a goal to increase revenue by a certain percentage or increase traffic to our websites. Normal and predictable goals.

Then David Ning shared his goal. He's the blogger behind the personal finance website, moneyning.com. He said, "I just want to get a little better each month." David's answer resonated with me, and I've made it my own goal in everything I do.

Unbeknownst to me at the time, the effectiveness of David's simple, humble goal was backed by mountains of research. Teresa Amabile is the Edsel Bryant Ford Professor of Business Administration and a Director of Research at Harvard Business School. She coauthored the book, *The Progress Principle*. In an article in *Harvard Business Review*, she tells the story of James Watson and Francis Crick.

Watson and Crick discovered the structure of DNA[38], for which they were awarded the Nobel Prize. Talk about a big goal. Yet they accomplished this big goal through a series of small wins, along with a healthy dose of small defeats. In studying their work, Professor Amabile found that their progress, or lack thereof, governed their emotions and motivation. A small win made them hungry for more.

As Professor Amabile wrote in the HBR article:

> "Of all the things that can boost emotions, motivation, and perceptions during a workday, the single most important is making progress in meaningful work. And the more frequently people experience that sense of progress, the more likely they are to be creatively productive in the long run. Whether they are trying to solve a major scientific mystery or simply produce a high-quality product or service, everyday progress—even a small win—can make all the difference in how they feel and perform."[39]

---

38 I should hasten to add that some would disagree with this claim, or at least be quick to give credit to Friedrich Miescher, Phoebus Levene, Erwin Chargaff, Rosalind Franklin and Maurice Wilkins. https://www.nature.com/scitable/topicpage/discovery-of-dna-structure-and-function-watson-397

39 https://hbr.org/2011/05/the-power-of-small-wins

The Progress Principle applies equally well to our journey to Level 7. The key is in our focus. If you are working hard to save 5% of your income, focusing on a goal of a 30% Saving Rate is not helpful. It may even be frustrating and discouraging. Every step will feel like a failure because it doesn't appear to get you closer to your goal. That's the last thing we want. So rather than focusing exclusively on your big goal, create smaller, intermediate goals to achieve. Perhaps for you it means increasing your Saving Rate from 5% to 7% within 12 months.

Achieving small wins has two concrete benefits. First, you increase your Saving Rate. While it may not seem like much at first, we now know how seemingly small changes, multiplied over time, have huge effects on our finances. Second, small wins encourage us to keep going. They show us that we can set goals, achieve them, and then keep moving toward bigger goals. **Small wins silence our inner voice that tries to convince us that we'll never succeed**.

If The Progress Principle can help two scientists discover the structure of DNA, it can help us achieve our Saving Rate goal. Here are some ideas to consider as you think about your small wins and next steps:

- Set your 401(k) to automatically increase your contributions by 1% a year (some 401(k) accounts offer this feature).
- Use one-half of your raise to increase your Saving Rate.
- Use one-half of your tax refund to increase your Saving Rate.

3 KEY CONCEPTS

1. Small wins enable us to focus on goals that are achievable in a reasonable amount of time.

2. Called The Progress Principle, seeing regular improvements, however small, builds our confidence and encourages us to keep moving toward bigger goals.

3. Think outside the box when it comes to small wins, such as saving one-half of your next raise or increasing your 401(k) contributions automatically.

CHAPTER 29

Debt

"Every time you borrow money, you're robbing your future self."
— Nathan W. Morris

Debt plays an important role in our journey to Financial Freedom. As you might guess, like running with weights in our pockets, debt slows us down. And a crushing amount of debt will bring us to our knees.

Over the next few chapters we are going to cover everything you need to know about debt. In this chapter, we will look at both the psychology and the math of debt. In the next chapter, we'll cover a powerfully effective way to get out of debt. And in our last chapter about debt, we'll look at whether you should tackle your debt *before* investing or invest while paying down your debt. In other words, we'll look at how to set financial priorities.

You may wonder why the chapters on debt appear here, separate from the sections on Financial Freedom and Saving Rate. To answer that question, I'm going to say something controversial. Having debt does not prevent you from achieving Financial Freedom. And having *no* debt does not guarantee Financial Freedom either.

Getting out of debt is an excellent goal. But it isn't THE goal. THE goal is Financial Freedom and ultimately Level 7. Debt can certainly get in the way. And oddly enough, paying off our debt can also help us develop the habits we need to achieve Financial Freedom at a young age.

Juggling multiple financial priorities is one of the trickiest questions in personal finance. Should you save for retirement or a down payment on a house? Should you fund your child's 529 plan or pay off your own school loans? And should you invest now or tackle all of your nonmortgage debt first?

These are important questions. As you might have guessed, I don't believe debt, in most cases, should stop you from investing. You'll see why over the next three chapters.

The 3 Problems with Debt

Debt causes us to spend more

It was 2005. I was listening to the Dave Ramsey show on the radio. I recall that there were two types of callers. The first called into the show with a heartbreaking story of financial ruin and seeking Dave's advice. The second type of caller was quite different. They called in to shout, "I'm debt-free." I decided then and there to be the second type of caller.

My wife and I didn't have soul-crushing debt; we weren't on the brink of bankruptcy. But we did have debt. We had credit card debt. We had school loans. We had a car loan. We had a home equity line of credit. And we had a mortgage. In many ways we were typical Americans pursuing the American Dream through debt-fueled living.

So I turned off the radio and took out a piece of paper. On that paper I wrote the following: "We will be totally debt-free by June 15, 2012." I gave us seven years to retire not only our nonmortgage debt, but our mortgage as well.

And then a month later we did the unthinkable. We decided to buy living room furniture. The furniture store offered us 0% financing for 12 months. What a deal. I turned it down and we paid cash. How could I turn down free money? If anything, I should take the deal, earn interest on the money from a savings account, and pay the debt off at the end of the year, right?

Not so fast. My concern was that if we financed the purchase, especially at 0%, we'd be tempted to buy more expensive furniture than what we could afford. Paying cash hurts. It affects how much we spend. So we paid cash. (I'm not opposed to using 0% balance transfer credit cards to help pay off existing debt. That's a different topic we'll cover in the next chapter.)

The first problem with debt is that financing a purchase often lulls us into spending more than we should. This is particularly true with cars and homes. That's not to say you shouldn't finance the purchase of a home. You should, however, be acutely aware of how financing the purchase is affecting your buying decision.

Debt limits our future

Imagine you are on a narrow trail. To your left is a forest so thick you can't turn off the path. To your immediate right is a sheer cliff with a 1,000-foot drop. That's what debt is like. Your options have been limited. You can't turn left or right. You must follow the narrow path ahead of debt and interest payments. One wrong turn and disaster awaits you.

Life without debt is like an open field. Where you go is totally up to you.

I've lived under both conditions. Trust me, the open field is where you want to be.

Debt is expensive

The third obvious problem with debt is the interest you pay. We've talked a lot about the power of compounding. We want the compounding to work *for* us, not against us. With the interest we pay on debt, our money is compounding for somebody else—our creditors.

Let's look at just how pernicious this reverse compounding can be when it comes to credit card debt. Let's imagine you've racked up $15,000 in credit card debt. The average interest rate on credit cards today is about 15%. Now guess what your minimum payment will be. The answer is stunning.

First, what would your payment be on a five-year, $15,000 car loan at 15%? Using a free calculator from the Internet, we see that the monthly payment is $356.85.

Now I know what you are asking. Who cares about a car payment when we are talking about credit card debt? Great question. I show you the car payment on a five-year loan to contrast it with the minimum credit card payment. Here it is—$300.

At first glance the two numbers don't seem that far apart. Just $56.85. It's here, however, that car loans and credit card debt part ways. A car loan is what the industry calls an installment loan. With the car payment, as with any installment loan, you'll continue to pay $356.85 each and every month until the debt is paid off. That's true even if you pay extra some months; the monthly payment never changes. The end result is that you pay off the car in five years, or earlier if you make extra payments along the way.

Credit card debt is different. The industry calls this type of debt *revolving debt*. Most credit card companies calculate the minimum monthly payment based on the outstanding balance. A standard formula uses 2% of the balance. That means as your balance goes down, so does your monthly payment. The effect of this formula, if you make only the minimum payment, is to significantly increase both the time it takes to pay off the debt and the total interest you'll pay.

Let's start with how long it will take. Using the credit card payoff calculator at financialmentor.com,[40] it will take (are you sitting down?) 44 years to pay off the debt.

It gets worse. The total interest paid will be a whopping $24,456.23. And that's on a debt of $15,000.

Some may think these numbers are impossible. I get it. So I grabbed one of my credit card statements that recently had a balance of $4,268.57 with an interest rate of 16.49%. I paid the card off in full, as I do every month. If I had made just the minimum payment of $42 (1% of the balance in this case) and continued making the minimum payment going forward, it would have taken me 17 years to pay it off and it would have cost me $9,368 in interest. How do I know this? The credit card issuer was kind enough to provide these details on the first page of my monthly statement.

---

40 https://financialmentor.com/calculator/credit-card-payoff-calculator

Credit card debt is like trying to run a race with a thumb tack in your shoe. In most cases we have nothing to show for the debt we've incurred as it often funds Lifestyle Expenses. Credit card issuers charge double-digit interest rates. And paying just the minimum payment each month guarantees you decades of payments that cost a fortune.

Good debt vs. Bad debt

You may have heard the concept of "good" debt and "bad" debt. Generally speaking, "good" debt is borrowing for something that can improve our finances. A home mortgage and school loans fit into this category. "Bad" debt is just about everything else.

There are several problems with the idea of good and bad debt. First, "good" debt can be very, very bad if taken to extremes. We've all heard of the family that bought far more home than they could afford, and then spent years barely getting by as they struggled to pay off the mortgage. And then there's the liberal arts major with $150,000 in school loans working at Starbucks. (I pick on liberal arts majors for two reasons. First, these degrees tend to qualify students for jobs that don't pay particularly well. Second, I majored in English.) So rather than trying to characterize debt as "good" or "bad," let's look at the major types of debt in some detail.

Debt to finance lifestyle

This usually comes in the form of credit card debt. We charge meals, entertainment, clothes, jewelry, electronics, and vacations. If we are living beyond our means, the debt grows as we are unable to pay it off each month.

The result is a mountain of credit card debt at double-digit interest rates. This is the worst kind of debt imaginable.

Car Loans

Car loans can seem like a fact of life. Everybody has a car loan, or two, or three, right? Well, no. We haven't had a car loan since 2005. Before that we didn't know any better.

The problem with a car loan is that it encourages us to buy more car than we can truly afford. We may be able to make the monthly payment. And I can assure you that the salesperson will be more than happy to help you calculate just what you can "afford" each month.

If you need to have a car, paying cash forces you to buy what you can truly afford.

Home Loans

A home mortgage is generally considered "good" debt. The reason is simple—homes tend to increase in value over the long term. This "good" debt, however, can quickly turn bad under several circumstances:

- You pay more than the value of the home (something that happened frequently just before the housing crash of 2007).
- You spend more on a home than you can truly afford.
- You finance almost all of the purchase price, leaving yourself few options should the value of the home drop and you need to sell.
- You buy in an area where renting is far more affordable.

Buying a home with a mortgage, while a reasonable choice under the right circumstances, can also be a big mistake.

School Loans

When I was growing up, a college degree was a ticket to the good life. Things have changed. Today the cost of a college education, particularly at private institutions, has skyrocketed. Tuition, room and board can easily approach $60,000 or more a year at some universities.

What's more, we must remember that a college degree, while valuable, is not a good deal at any price, and that not all degrees have the same value. For example, an engineering degree has more economic value than a liberal arts degree. (As I noted above, I was an English major. I'm not picking on liberal arts degrees, but the fact is that other degrees enable you to get a job making a lot more money.)

Before we take on a student loan, we need to have a plan regarding how we will pay for it. This in turn means understanding the types of jobs that our education will qualify us for and how much money we are likely to make. As a rule of thumb, *we should not borrow more than one to one-and-a-half times our expected first year income*. Consider that before you sign the loan documents.

How Debt Affects Your Wealth

Let's return to the example from my own credit card statement. Recall that I had a balance of $4,268.57. At that point, if I had made just the minimum payment, it would have taken me 17 years to pay it off and it would have cost me $9,368 in interest. What is the true impact on our wealth with this credit card debt?

First, had we invested the $4,268.57 instead of taking a vacation (or buying clothes, jewelry or electronics), it would have grown to $20,618.40 over the 17-year period assuming a 9.3% return.

Now let's look at those pesky interest payments. While we'd pay more interest in the earlier months when the balance was higher, let's just divide the interest payments equally over the 17 years. The result is $45.92 a month in interest. If we had invested that amount over 17 years, we would have added another $22,695.05 to our net worth.

In total, the $4,268.57 credit card debt reduced our net worth by $43,313.45 at the end of 17 years. And the cost only goes up when we look further into the future. That's an expensive vacation.

Debt and Your Level 7 Journey

Earlier in this chapter I said that paying off debt can help you develop the habits needed to achieve Financial Freedom at a young age. Let's take a closer look at this.

Recall the hypothetical income we've used before:

- Annual Income: $75,000
- Saving Rate: 20% ($15,000 a year)
- Spending Rate: 80% ($60,000 a year)

In previous chapters, we haven't looked too closely at just how this person is spending $60,000 a year. For much of what we've discussed, the answer didn't matter. Now it does.

Let's assume that $1,000 a month goes to nonmortgage debt. These debts might include school loans, a car payment, and perhaps credit card debt. That's a lot of money. It also means that our hypothetical Financial Freedom Fighter isn't actually spending $60,000 a year on current purchases. $12,000 of that amount is going to pay for purchases made in the past on credit.

Perhaps the above numbers make more sense this way:

- Annual Income: $75,000
- Saving Rate: 20% ($15,000 a year)
- Spending Rate: 64% ($48,000 a year)
- Debt Service: 16% ($12,000 a year)

Why is this important? For two reasons. First, it shows us that this person has managed to live on 64% of their income. True, they can't save all of the rest. Sixteen percent is going to debt payments. But they've still demonstrated their ability to live far below their means.

Second, eventually that debt is going to be paid off. When that happens, they can immediately ratchet up their Saving Rate to 36%. Even if they decided to spend some of that difference, say 6%, they could still increase their Saving Rate to 30%.

Recall how increasing our Saving Rate has a Slingshot Effect. We've not only increased our savings, but we've also decreased our spending. The exact same thing happens when we pay off debt and take the money we were using on payments and start saving it instead.

And that raises an important question: How do we pay off our debt? In the next chapter we'll walk through a simple system that will do just that.

3 KEY CONCEPTS

1. Debt doesn't make achieving Financial Freedom impossible, but it does make it harder.

2. There is a silver lining. Once your debt is paid off, your monthly expenses go down while your Saving Rate goes up.

3. Be careful to avoid too much "good" debt. Buying a home and getting an education are reasonable goals. Financing them with too much debt, however, can have lifelong consequences.

CHAPTER 30

How to Get Out of Debt

"Rather go to bed supperless, than rise in debt."

– Benjamin Franklin

Getting out of debt is simple. Note that I didn't say it was easy. But it is simple. Here are the four steps:

1. Stop going into more debt.
2. Get rid of debt.
3. Refinance debt.
4. Pay down debt (debt snowball vs. debt avalanche).

Let's look at each step.

Step 1: *Stop* Going into More Debt

Feel free to call me Captain Obvious. Yet this is by far the hardest and most important part of becoming debt-free.

My wife and I struggled with this step for years. While we never had overwhelming debt, it was like a low-grade fever. It didn't kill us, but it didn't feel good either. We had school loans, credit card debt, car loans, a mortgage, and a home equity line of credit.

So how do you stop going into more debt?

First, you have to zero in on your weakness. What types of debt do you struggle with? Does it add up slowly over time with small purchases on a credit card? Or is your day-to-day spending in control, but you make big purchases periodically that get you into trouble.

Second, once you've identified your weak points, address them. For credit card debt, one option is to cut up the credit cards. You don't even need to close the account (which can hurt your credit score if you do). Just cut up the cards so you can't use them. The key is to remove the need to rely on your willpower.

In some cases, debt is the result of poor planning. Many people have no idea how they spend their money each month. They are surprised when their line of credit at the bank has to cover debit card purchases they've made near the end of the month. Others may do a great job of planning their everyday expenses but then get blindsided by the car insurance bill that comes every six months.

Here's the thing. People get into debt a million different ways. But there's only one way to get out of debt. And it begins with *avoiding new debt*.

Step 2: Get Rid of Debt

The second step is one that a lot of people miss. Before we begin mapping out a plan to pay down our debt, we should first decide if we have any debts we can eliminate *immediately*. How?

There are two kinds of debt. The first kind of debt is used to buy an asset. A mortgage or car loan comes to mind. The second kind of debt is everything else. Whether it's financing a vacation on a credit card or borrowing to go to school, the result is the same: we don't have a physical asset we can sell to pay off the debt.

Here's the point. Examine all of your debts. If you have borrowed to buy something you can now sell, consider whether you should sell it. This question most often involves the purchase of a car.

Now, as you know, I'm not here to tell you to sell your car. If you recently bought a new car, the depreciation in value has likely left you underwater (i.e., the amount of debt is greater than the value of the car). That doesn't mean you shouldn't sell it, by the way. But I understand it presents an issue to consider.

What I am here to say is that you should *consider* selling anything that you purchased on credit. The result may be that you decide not to sell anything. Others may decide that their $30,000 car is not as important as achieving Financial Freedom, and they sell it.

The point is to at least consider the option. Remember to always ask "What if?"

Step 3: Refinance Debt

The third step is a no-brainer. We want to lower the interest rate on every debt that we can. Many people are familiar with refinancing a mortgage for a lower rate. But you can refinance *any* debt. Look at each debt you have and evaluate whether you can refinance at a lower rate. Here are some ideas and resources to consider:

Mortgage/HELOC: For a mortgage or home equity line of credit (HELOC), LendingTree is a great way to compare multiple financing options in one place. You can also ask your current mortgage company what rates they offer.

Car Loans: If you decide to keep your car, see if you can get a lower rate on the loan. Once again, LendingTree is a good option for comparing rates.

Credit Card Debt: If you have high interest credit card debt, consider transferring it to a card that offers a 0% APR introductory rate. Today's 0% offers last for up to 21 months. Keep in mind that you'll pay a balance transfer fee of 3% in most cases. This is well worth it if you are transferring debt that currently costs you 15% or more.

Student Loans: Student loans come in two varieties—federal loans and private loans. In both cases, if you want to refinance the debt to a lower interest rate, the resulting loan will be a private loan. Federal loans cannot be refinanced to a lower rate with another federal loan. (Federal loans can be consolidated, but the interest rate of the new loan is an average of the federal loans you consolidated.)

Why do I make this point? Because federal loans come with some advantages that private loans do not. In some situations federal loans can be forgiven. And federal loans offer repayment options that private loans don't offer. The point is this: before refinancing a federal loan into a lower rate private loan, evaluate whether the loss of these advantages is worth the lower rate.

With that said, here are some excellent sources for refinancing student loans:

- SoFi
- CommonBond
- Laurel Road

You'll also find more refinancing options at Student Loan Hero.

Step 4: Pay Down Debt (Debt Snowball vs. Debt Avalanche)

Now we get to actually tackling our debt. Here we have to answer two critical questions:

1. How much money will we put towards our debt each month?
2. If the amount is more than the minimum payments, which debt do we apply the extra money to?

Let's look at each question.

1. How Much?

How much money you should put toward your debt will vary from person to person. Some will struggle to pay just the minimum. Others will have more flexibility but struggle with deciding on financial priorities.

In addition to paying down debt, other priorities may include one or more of the following:

- Saving and investing toward your Financial Freedom.

- Saving a down payment for a home.
- Saving for a child's education.

How do you decide what to do? First, recognize that there is no one "right" answer to this question. Imagine one person with credit card debt at 0% interest. Now imagine another person with credit card debt at 27% interest. Their financial priorities are vastly different.

Generally speaking, you should consider the following factors when setting your financial priorities:

- **The interest rate on your debt**. The higher the rate, the more paying down that debt becomes a financial priority. Anything above 10% should be a priority.
- **Retirement matching**. Many employers match 401(k) contributions. If you're lucky enough to have this benefit, contributing enough to your 401(k) to take full advantage of the match should be a financial priority.
- **Emergency fund**. Saving one month of expenses, at a minimum, should be a financial priority. We need this breathing room to handle emergencies or a loss of income.

2. Which Debt?

Assuming you can pay more than the minimum payment on your debts, you now need to decide which debt to apply the extra payment to. There are two schools of thought on this question. One is called the debt snowball. The other is called the debt avalanche.

- **Debt Snowball**: The first school of thought recommends applying extra payments to *the debt with the smallest balance*, regardless of the interest rate. The argument goes that paying off a debt completely will help motivate us to continue paying down our debt. By focusing on the debt with the smallest balance, you'll pay it off faster than you would debts with larger balances. Recall The Progress Principle.

- **Debt Avalanche**: The second school of thought recommends focusing on *the debt with the highest interest rate*. By paying down high interest rate debt first, you get out of debt faster and cheaper than with the debt snowball approach.

So who is right? Well, there is research that supports the Debt Snowball approach. According to one study described in *Harvard Business Review*, "'Pay the smallest debt first' is a straightforward strategy that can be easily communicated and easily applied—and that's sorely needed by millions of American credit card users."

At the same time, math doesn't lie. Depending on your interest rates, the Debt Snowball method could cost you thousands in extra interest payments and significantly lengthen the time it takes you to pay off your debts.

Ultimately you should do what works for you. The goal is to get out of debt. If paying the smallest balance first helps you accomplish your goal, so be it. If you can tackle the highest rate debt first, all the better.

I recommend that you calculate the difference between these two approaches. It's easy to do with this free Debt Snowball Calculator.[41]

---

41 https://tools.doughroller.net/debt-snowball-calculator

3 KEY CONCEPTS

1. Debt, like an anchor around your neck while you try to swim, makes achieving Financial Freedom hard.

2. The first and most important step to getting out of debt is to stop taking on any new debt.

3. As important as paying off your debt is, you should never ignore your other financial goals.

Take Action: Using the information in this chapter, map out a debt repayment plan. Put in place steps to keep from going into more debt (cut up those cards if you must). Evaluate whether you should get rid of any debt. Then consider refinancing some or all of your remaining debt. And finally, tackle your debt with either the debt snowball or debt avalanche method.

CHAPTER 31

Priorities

"Avoiding new debt is vastly more important than
how fast you pay off your existing debt."

– Me

One of the toughest questions in all personal finance relates to priorities. We are generally faced with multiple financial goals, not just one. We want to save for our child's education, and a down payment for a home, and for retirement. At the same time we want to pay off school loans and credit card debt. And then there is saving for emergencies. Where do we start and what should be our number one priority?

What makes these choices so difficult is that we don't know the future. We don't know what the stock market will do tomorrow, never mind years from now. We don't know what our income will be in the future. We don't know when the car will break down, or when the furnace will stop working. We may think we know the future, and then a health issue changes everything.

So how do we decide? In this chapter my goal is to convince you that, in most cases, debt should not stop us from investing. We'll dig into the numbers, but first, let's cover three important concepts related to personal finance.

Concept #1: Begin with the End in Mind

Stephen Covey's bestselling book, *The 7 Habits of Highly Effective People*, is a must read. The second habit in his book is to begin with the end in mind. As we are making decisions in life, we should always be mindful of our ultimate goal. Lose sight of your goal and you become like a ship's captain who is sailing at night and has lost his way.

Our goal is Financial Freedom that empowers us to live a meaningful life. Our goal is not to be debt-free. While that can certainly be part of the process, it doesn't guarantee Financial Freedom.

I worked as an attorney in Washington, DC for 25 years. Over that time, I grew accustomed to the homeless asking for money. One day a middle-aged man who clearly had lived a hard life asked me for some change. Instead of giving him money, I took him to a Burger King on K Street and paid for his lunch. It's reasonable to believe that this man didn't have any debt. He also didn't have Financial Freedom.

The takeaway here is NOT that debt doesn't matter. Debt is a huge financial obstacle for countless people. But we shouldn't elevate getting out of debt as our #1 priority to the exclusion of all other financial goals simply because debt is "bad."

Concept #2: Multiple Goals are the Norm

I've received countless emails from podcast listeners asking about financial priorities. A common question is whether they should pay off all of their debt or start investing for retirement. My response is typically, "Yes. Do both."

There's no rule that requires us to tackle one financial priority at a time. The problem is that many financial gurus talk in terms of eight or 10 or 12 steps to Financial Freedom. When we think in these terms, we lock ourselves into a rigid and often suboptimal plan. We must save an emergency fund of a certain amount. Then we must pay off all of our debt. Only then can we start investing.

Nonsense.

There may be times when we should focus on just one financial priority. Often, however, we should be tackling several goals at one time. That may mean adding to our emergency fund each month while we also pay extra on credit cards. And at the same time we may be adding to our 401(k) at work to take advantage of our employer's matching contributions.

Concept #3: There is No Single Right Answer

A number of personal finance gurus promote "rules of thumb." One of the most destructive rules of thumb is that everybody should always pay off all nonmortgage debt before investing. Let's put this rule of thumb to the test.

Imagine a recent college graduate with $75,000 in student loans at 6% interest. Let's further assume that if they manage their money perfectly and focus exclusively on paying off this debt while ignoring all other financial goals, they can be debt-free in five years.

Now, let's also imagine that their employer matches 401(k) contributions dollar for dollar up to 6% of their salary. What should they do? If they blindly follow the rule of thumb, they will forego a 6% company match for five years. They might as well take their cash, set it in the driveway, pour gas on it, and set it on fire. It would be insane to forego this company match so that you can focus on long-term debt that is costing just 6%.

On the other hand, some people have significant credit card debt with interest rates of 25% or more. In that case, assuming they can't lower the interest rate on their credit cards, they probably should focus exclusively on paying off this high-interest debt before investing.

There's a reason why we call it **personal** finance. It's not one-size-fits-all.

Why Investing Is More Important than Paying Off Debt

In most cases, investing should not take a backseat to paying off debt. That's not to say you shouldn't make more than the minimum payments on your debt. Generally, however, tackling your debt shouldn't come at the expense of saving and investing.

There are five reasons why.

Reason #1: The Match

As I noted above, many companies will match a portion of your 401(k) contributions. If that is the case, you should work hard to contribute, at a minimum, enough to take full advantage of that match. Let's look at an example.

Let's assume you make $75,000 a year and your company matches 50 cents on the dollar up to 6% of your income. Six percent of $75,000 is $4,500. Since the employer in our example matches 50 cents on the dollar (some match dollar for dollar), you'll receive an extra $2,250 if you contribute 6% of your salary to the 401(k). The result is an annual contribution of $6,750 ($4,500 you contribute + $2,250 employer match).

On top of this, you'll get a tax break for your $4,500 contribution (we are assuming a traditional 401(k), not a Roth, in this example). While that benefit will depend on your tax situation, we'll assume you save 25% between state and federal income tax, or $1,125 ($4,500 x 25%). The result is that your after-tax paycheck is reduced by $3,375 a year, or $281.25 a month.

Now let's go down the rabbit hole. We'll also assume you have $75,000 in school loans at 6% over ten years. Using this handy loan calculator (http://www.bankrate.com/calculators/mortgages/loan-calculator.aspx), your monthly payments total $832.65. Pay that amount each month and your school loans will be history in a decade.

We could, however, forego the 401(k) contribution and direct our extra money to the school loans. If we did that, we'd have an extra $281.25 a month to throw at the loans. We would have no 401(k) savings and we'd lose the company match. Following this approach, we'd pay off our school loans in about seven years.

Now let's compare.

Pay off School Loans and Then Invest

As noted above, it would take us seven years to pay off our school loans if that were our #1 priority. If we then started investing $4,500 in our 401(k), we'd have $23,253.85 three years later (assuming the company match and a 9.3% return). The net result is that after ten years, we'd have our school loans paid off and about $23,200 saved in our 401(k). We'd also avoid about three years of school loan payments, adding about $34,400 to our savings (again, assuming a 9.3% return). The net result is about $58,000 saved.

Contribute $4,500/Year to our 401(k) While Making the Minimum Payment on our School Loans

If we instead contributed $4,500 each year to our 401(k), it would take us the full ten years to pay off our school loans. During that time, however, our 401(k) balance would grow to $110,717.32, thanks in part to the company match.

> **The Point**: Because of the company match, tax savings on a 401(k), and the relatively low rate on our school loans, it's far better to contribute to our 401(k) rather than focusing exclusively on our debt.

I know I've thrown a lot of numbers at you in this section. We could have gone even further. Perhaps the interest on your student loans is deductible, lowering the effective interest rate you are paying. This would further favor contributing to your 401(k). Perhaps you contribute to a Roth 401(k), which would change the numbers. The key is that an employer-match to your 401(k) is a terrible thing to waste. It's even worse if you lose the benefit of that match because you blindly follow some rule of thumb.

Reason #2: Use It or Lose It

Even without a company match, investing in a 401(k), an IRA, or both, should be a priority. These accounts limit the amount you can contribute each year. In 2019, the limit on 401(k) contributions is $19,000 and the limit on an IRA contribution is $6,000 (those 50 or older also have catch-up contributions).

Here's the key. You can't go back in time to make contributions for years that you missed. If you don't contribute anything to your 401(k) this year, the opportunity is lost forever. The contribution limits reset each year. Given the significant tax advantage these retirement accounts offer, we should take advantage of them to the best of our ability each and every year.

Reason #3: Habit

For many people, saving money is hard at first. Like developing any good habit, it takes time. Eventually, we save and invest money without giving it much thought. But at first it's like using a muscle we haven't used for some time. It hurts.

We shouldn't let our savings muscle atrophy for years while we tackle our debt. And I would argue that developing the habit of saving will actually help us develop the habit of living debt-free. Seeing our savings and investments grow can help motivate us to improve other areas of our finances.

The experience of investing *early* also helps us develop the skill to survive bad markets. The sooner we learn this the better.

Reason #4: Reality

Like dieting, paying off debt is often a "two steps forward, one step back" adventure. You have some success for several months, and then something comes along that causes you to buy something on credit. It would be great if we could handle our finances perfectly and never go into more debt, but that's not the reality for a lot of people.

The result is that it can take longer to get out of debt than we had planned. At one level that's just fine. We all make mistakes, financial and otherwise. As long as we recognize the mistakes we make and get back on track, we will eventually reach our goals.

The problem comes when we've held off investing while paying off our debt. We may have had a five-year plan to be debt-free, but what happens when that plan turns into eight, or ten, or even 15 years? Will we avoid investing while we stumble through our efforts to get out of debt?

As Mike Tyson said, "Everybody has a plan until they get punched in the mouth." The same is true with getting out of debt. Continue working hard to pay off your debts, of course. But don't delay investing.

Reason #5: Time

The final reason is time. As we've discussed, building wealth takes time. The sooner you start putting your dollars to work, the better. As you set your own financial priorities, keep a few things in mind.

First, there are always exceptions to the exceptions to the exceptions. As an example, federal student loans have unique features. You may be on a plan that results in forgiveness of a significant portion of your debt. Or perhaps you are on an income-contingent repayment plan. If so, these must be factored into your overall financial plan. They may not fit neatly into a "rule of thumb" or into my list of financial priorities.

Second, Financial Freedom is not just about the numbers. While that's the primary focus of this book, there is an entire field of behavioral finance. While

I believe you should work to tackle debt with rates above 10%, you might not be comfortable with *any* debt. If your 8% debt is keeping you awake at night, that's a problem you need to address now. Don't push it down the list of priorities because of anything you read in this or any other personal finance book.

Finally, things change. I've drawn a line at 10% interest on debt. Yes, it's arbitrary. It's also based on today's low rate environment. I'm old enough to remember when 10% debt would have been a steal. At that time (early 80s) I was earning 15% on short-term CDs.

The point is there is no always-correct-for-everybody list of financial priorities. Learn as much as you can, and then make the best decisions for your specific circumstances.

3 KEY CONCEPTS

1. While paying off debt is an important financial priority, saving and investing should be our #1 priority.

2. Giving up an employer match to your 401(k) is a costly mistake.

3. Avoiding new debt is vastly more important than how fast you pay off your existing debt.

CHAPTER 32

Yes, but…

"I attribute my success to this:—I never gave or took an excuse."
– Florence Nightingale

M y goal here is simple: To convince you to start saving and investing today. Not tomorrow, next week, or next month. Today. In the last chapter, we discussed why debt should not stop us from investing. In this chapter, we are going to cover other common objections I've heard over the years.

Here I should add that every situation is different. There are certainly some extreme cases where an individual or family simply can't start investing today. I'm going to go out on a limb, however, and assert that most people reading this book are capable of investing something, anything, today.

With that said, here are the common objections I hear regarding investing.

I have too Little to Invest

We now know the power of investing small amounts of money over time. Yet many believe that, as much as they'd like to start investing, they don't have enough money. This is simply not true. You don't need to have a lot of money to start investing. In fact, you can begin with as little as $25 or less a month.

Most 401(k) plans do not have minimum contribution amounts. There are also a number of investing services that don't require a minimum contribution amount. *Betterment* is one of them. The key to remember is that you can start investing with just a few dollars a month.

If nothing else, start by putting your money in an online savings account. You won't earn much interest, but that's not the point. Once you save $1,000, you can invest in a Vanguard target date retirement fund. The point is this: you don't need a lot of money to start investing.

I'm too Young

Given what we now know about the power of time, it's hard to believe that anyone would actually raise this objection. But they do. Investing seems like something "old" people do. In fact, many young people don't even think about investing. It's not that they consider it and decide to wait. They don't even consider it.

As we've seen, even small amounts of money can turn into a big pile of wealth. For that reason, I firmly believe investing should begin in high school. I had part time jobs starting in ninth grade and I so wish that I would have started investing then.

I've had the opportunity to work with young people just out of high school. These were friends of ours, and they wanted to know how to invest. One who comes to mind is Stephen. He was a freshman in college and one day he and his father stopped by my office (which is a workshop in our house). We discussed many of the things in this book. Following our conversation, Stephen opened an account at Vanguard, and he invested some of the money he'd saved working part-time jobs in a Vanguard target date retirement fund. He's on his way to Financial Freedom.

The key is to see yourself as an investor, regardless of your age. Investing isn't for old people. Investing is for anybody, at any age, who wants to take control of their money and achieve Financial Freedom. The sooner you start, the easier it is.

I'm too Old

Some people believe that they are too late and that it won't make a difference. They regret financial decisions they made years earlier, and they have convinced themselves that saving and investing in the twilight of their lives is pointless. But you're never too old to save and invest.

It reminds me of a conversation I had with my mom. She was in her forties and thinking about finishing her college degree. She wondered if she was too old to go back to school. My response was simple, "Mom, in a few years you'll be 50. You can either be 50 with a college degree or 50 without one. The choice is yours."

She got her degree, followed by a 20+ year career in teaching.

I don't have an Emergency Fund

An emergency fund is an important part of sound money management. The unexpected happens repeatedly in life. Whether it's the car that breaks down or the furnace that stops working, it almost never happens at a convenient time. It's therefore important to set money aside in a savings account for emergencies.

If you are literally starting with no savings, focus on building an emergency fund first. You may have heard the rule of thumb that one should have an emergency fund equal to three to six months' worth of expenses. I have no objection to this rule of thumb, but don't treat it like Gospel. My wife and I keep an entire year's worth of expenses in savings. Every situation is different.

If you are just starting out, spend the next six months saving an emergency fund. At the end of six months, reevaluate your situation, and consider taking some of your future earnings and contributing to your 401(k) at work (particularly if your employer matches your contributions) or an IRA. Remember that we can and often should tackle two or more financial priorities at the same time. It's not all or nothing.

And that brings us to the next objection.

First, I need to Save for a Home (or a Car, or My Child's Education)

Most times in my life I've been faced with multiple financial goals. These goals have included the following:

- Saving for a down payment on a house.
- Paying off credit card debt.
- Paying off school loans.
- Funding 529 plans for the children's education.
- Saving for a vacation.
- Saving for a home remodel.
- Paying off the mortgage.
- Saving for retirement.

It's rare that we have only one financial goal. With that said, saving to build wealth and achieve Financial Freedom should be our number one goal. That doesn't mean we ignore all of our other financial goals. We can put money to multiple goals each month. But your eye should be on Financial Freedom first.

I Don't Know How

The last objection is perhaps the easiest to address. Investing is simple. It may seem mysterious now. You may be confused by all of the terminology (e.g., asset allocation, small cap stocks, mutual funds vs. ETFs, etc.), but don't let the language of investing scare you.

We've covered investing in Part IV. You now know that you can build a great portfolio with a single mutual fund. Or if you want to get crazy, you can use the 3-Fund Portfolio. No excuses.

3 KEY CONCEPTS

1. Your objections to saving and investing are common. At first, just about everybody has objections, but it's critical to your future that you work through them.

2. Remember that "the obstacle is the way."[42] Find what's keeping you from investing and run toward it.

3. You'll have many financial goals throughout your life. Investing to achieve Financial Freedom should be first.

---

42 https://www.amazon.com/Obstacle-Way-Timeless-Turning-Triumph/dp/1591846358

CHAPTER 33

To Level 7 and Beyond!

"It is not the critic who counts; not the man who points out how the strong man stumbles, or where the doer of deeds could have done them better. The credit belongs to the man who is actually in the arena, whose face is marred by dust and sweat and blood; who strives valiantly; who errs, who comes short again and again, because there is no effort without error and shortcoming; but who does actually strive to do the deeds; who knows great enthusiasms, the great devotions; who spends himself in a worthy cause; who at the best knows in the end the triumph of high achievement, and who at the worst, if he fails, at least fails while daring greatly, so that his place shall never be with those cold and timid souls who neither know victory nor defeat."

– Theodore Roosevelt

You've come a long way. And yet your journey is just beginning. You're like Bilbo Baggins leaving the Shire to go on a great adventure.

My journey started later in life. It wasn't until about the age of 40 that I took the red pill. Before then I saw money as something to spend on stuff. It never occurred to me that I could use money to buy the most precious gift—Financial Freedom.

I've often wondered what caused me to see money differently. We didn't suffer a financial crisis. I didn't have a near-death experience. Yet one day I found myself asking a deceptively profound question: What if?

What if I could be just as happy with less stuff? What if I could have complete control over what made me happy and what didn't make me happy? What if the things I thought were making me happy really weren't? Even worse, what if they made life less joyful?

These questions in turn caused me to focus on those things in my life that I could control. Money was one of them. My health was another.

My hope is that this book has caused you to question some of your own beliefs about money and happiness. Yes, you can retire early with what you've learned in this book. The secret behind this book, however, is that it's not about early retirement. It's about Financial Freedom. Once you achieve it, what you do with that freedom is up to you.

Whether you are in your twenties or thirties and want to retire early, or are in your forties or fifties and want to retire "on time," my hope for you is that, in the words of Teddy Roosevelt, you dare greatly. Ask profound "What if" questions. Run 21-day experiments. Start saving and investing today, even if it's just $25 a month. And whatever you do, don't end your days knowing "neither victory nor defeat."

Next Steps

1. Check out my resources page: www.retirebeforemomanddad.com resources. Here I list books, software, and apps I recommend for everything from budgeting to investing to improving your credit. And I keep this page updated as new tools and books come out.

2. Be sure to watch the videos I've created to cover many of the topics in this book.

3. Visit the Dough Roller Facebook Group: www.doughroller.net/facebookgroup. We are more than 6,000 Freedom Fighters helping each other out as we each make our way to Level 7.

4. Visit my personal blog at robberger.com, where I write about upcoming books, running an online business, productivity hacks and life goals.

Index

Acknowledgments

My wife, Victoria, has managed to survive this life with me by her side for nearly 31 years and counting. For that alone she deserves a medal. She supported the development of this book and patiently listened to me as I no doubt bored her about expense ratios, money audits, and the 4% Rule. Thank you.

In 2013 I started the Dough Roller Money Podcast. Almost immediately my inbox was flooded with email messages asking about everything from budgeting to investing. In response, I started a Facebook Group where folks could ask and answer questions about money. Today nearly 7,000 members are helping each other achieve Financial Freedom.

This group helped me, too. They held me accountable as I wrote this book. I'm forever grateful.

Cortlon Cofield of Cofield Advisors gave me a swift kick in the butt when I needed it most. His encouragement helped me get this book across the finish line.

The team at Book Launchers helped me in countless ways, including editing, editing and editing. Their editing was also invaluable.

There have been countless personal finance bloggers who have helped me in more ways than they know. To name any would be to unintentionally exclude others, but such is life:

Phillip Taylor (ptmoney.com and finconexpo.com)

David Weliver (moneyunder30.com)

Ryan Guina (cashmoneylife.com and themilitarywallet.com)

J.D. Roth (getrichslowly.org)

Jeff Rose (goodfinancialcents.com)

Jim Wang (wallethacks.com)

Larry Ludwig (larryludwig.com)

Robert Farrington (thecollegeinvestor.com)

Todd Tresidder (financialmentor.com)

Bob Lotich (christianpf.com)

Steve Chou (mywifequitherjob.com)

Greg Go (wisebread.com)

Tom Drake (maplemoney.com)

Janet Novack, my boss at Forbes, took time out of her crazy schedule to read a draft of this book. She was, as she always is, brutally kind.

Last but not least, I'd like to thank my mom. Her love and support has never wavered, even when I forget to call.